ROYAL
PROGRESS

DISCARDED
ROYAL
PROGRESS

Canada's Monarchy in the Age of Disruption

═EDITED BY═

D. MICHAEL JACKSON

FOREWORD BY THE HON. MARGARET MCCAIN, CC, ONB

DUNDURN
TORONTO

Publisher: Scott Fraser | Acquiring editor: Kathryn Lane | Editor: Dominic Farrell
Designer: Laura Boyle
Cover image: Courtesy Hon. Serge Joyal

Printer: Marquis Book Printing Inc.

Library and Archives Canada Cataloguing in Publication

Title: Royal progress : Canada's monarchy in the age of disruption / edited by D. Michael Jackson ; foreword by the Hon. Margaret McCain, CC, ONB.
Names: Jackson, D. Michael, editor.
Description: Includes bibliographical references.
Identifiers: Canadiana (print) 20200151592 | Canadiana (ebook) 20200151657 | ISBN 9781459745735 (softcover) | ISBN 9781459745742 (PDF) | ISBN 9781459745759 (EPUB)
Subjects: LCSH: Monarchy—Canada. | LCSH: Canada—Foreign relations—Great Britain. | LCSH: Great Britain—Foreign relations—Canada.
Classification: LCC FC246.M6 R69 2020 | DDC 320.471—dc23

We acknowledge the support of the Canada Council for the Arts and the Ontario Arts Council for our publishing program. We also acknowledge the financial support of the Government of Ontario, through the Ontario Book Publishing Tax Credit and Ontario Creates, and the Government of Canada.

VISIT US AT

 dundurn.com | @dundurnpress | dundurnpress | dundurnpress

Dundurn
3 Church Street, Suite 500
Toronto, Ontario, Canada
M5E 1M2

Dedicated to **John Fraser, CM**
Founding President of the Institute for the Study of the Crown in
Canada at Massey College, in recognition of his leadership in establishing
Her Majesty's third Canadian Chapel Royal *Gi-Chi-Twaa Gimaa Kwe,
Mississauga Anishinaabek AName Gamik* "The Queen's Anishinaabek
Sacred Place" at Massey College, Toronto, honouring the historic
relationship between Indigenous Peoples and the Crown.

CONTENTS

FOREWORD

Margaret McCain

During the summer of 2019, the Institute for the Study of the Crown in Canada at Massey College held its fourth conference on the Crown. For two intensive days at the University of Toronto, scholars and students of the Crown in Canada presented, discussed, and debated not just the role of the Crown in Canada's system of governance, but its evolution and future, as well as the distinctive colouring the Canadian Crown has taken on through the years. Scholars from the United Kingdom, Australia, and New Zealand made contributions of their own based on their unique experiences of the Crown.

I was delighted to be the honorary chair of the conference, just as I am to be patron of the Institute itself. This is for some obvious reasons, but also for some not-quite-so-obvious reasons, too! The obvious ones are … *well … obvious*: I love our Queen. She is the most hard-working sovereign in our history. She loves Canada and has visited it more than any other Commonwealth country outside her home base in the United Kingdom. I once had the privilege to be her representative in New Brunswick as her lieutenant governor. It was the honour of a lifetime and cemented a commitment I will always support.

The not-so-obvious reasons have to do with important defining concepts of our Constitution.

The Crown and the way it has evolved in Canada help define who we are. It is an institution at the heart of our country's history and continuing experience, but one often taken for granted. As was made clear in the conference, this may be changing. Just one example: the historic relationship between the Crown and the Indigenous Peoples of this land, while not without its challenges, nevertheless holds out a promise to bring concrete reality to reconciliation.

Another is the way governments and government institutions deal and communicate with each other. When I was lieutenant governor in New Brunswick, I knew I had a special responsibility to represent both the Acadian French-speaking population and the majority English-speaking population. The modern Crown sets standards of civility and decency in all its relations that are reminders of the way we should operate between institutions and with the general public. The fact that our Institute takes regular stock of the institution of the Crown is its biggest service to Canada.

This conference was important for many reasons, but perhaps the most important in my mind was that it brought together people who believe that Canada and the Crown have a joint mission to protect and serve this good land. A joint mission, if you like, to buttress its strengths as well as help heal its wounds; to help us prepare for a future where our willingness to marry the best of the past and present into a coherent path toward the future is a tangible goal.

I am so pleased that some of the work of the conference is reflected in this publication, together with essays from other equally qualified authors. I extend my congratulations and thanks to all who contributed to the conference and this volume. The work is important because the Canadian story is important.

PREFACE

D. Michael Jackson

I n 2019, the Institute for the Study of the Crown in Canada at Massey College convened its fourth conference on the Crown, occurring for the first time at its home base in the University of Toronto. The previous ones had taken place in Ottawa (2010), Regina (2012), and Victoria (2016). This latest conference, entitled The Crown in a Time of Transition, included speakers from Canada, Australia, New Zealand, and the United Kingdom. The presentations — and the lively discussions that followed each — were grouped under five topics: the Crown and Indigenous Peoples, the reserve powers of the Crown, the succession to the throne, the viceregal offices, and "moving toward a new reign." The present volume covers these topics except for that of the reserve powers.

Of the nine chapters, six are based on papers given at the conference. Chapters 1, 2, and 7 were generously contributed by other authors.

A welcome feature of the 2019 conference was its timely emphasis on the relationship of the Crown with Indigenous Peoples — the first topic in the present book, just as it was the first session at the conference. That session was preceded by a historic gathering at Massey College of senior Indigenous leaders with the Canadian viceregal representatives — the governor general, lieutenant governors, and territorial commissioners. National Chief Perry Bellegarde of the Assembly of First Nations delivered a keynote address to the gathering in Massey's Chapel Royal, designated by the Queen in 2017 as Canada's third chapel royal and allied to the Mississaugas of the Credit First Nation. We are grateful to Chief Bellegarde for agreeing to include an edited version of his address in this book.

Another welcome feature of the conference in Toronto was a panel discussion by three former lieutenant governors, who gave their personal perspectives on the provincial viceregal office — a "real life" counterpoint to the academic presentations.[1] It was fitting that one of them was the first Indigenous lieutenant governor in his province and another the most recent viceregal representative in Canada to exercise the reserve power of declining ministerial advice.

We are grateful to another former lieutenant governor, the Honourable Margaret McCain, the Queen's representative in New Brunswick from 1994 to 1997, for serving as honorary chair of the 2019 conference and now as patron of the Institute for the Study of the Crown in Canada at Massey College. In both capacities she kindly contributed the foreword to this book.

The Institute expresses its appreciation to the Honourable Margaret McCain, the Honourable Henry Jackman, Dr. Eric Jackman, and the Tovell-Ostry Fund at Massey College for their generous donations, which made the conference, and ultimately this book, feasible. We also gratefully acknowledge Massey College and Trinity College, our hosts at the University of Toronto, whose staff made us welcome in facilities ideally suited to a conference of this kind. As always, John Fraser, founding president of the Institute for the Study of the Crown in Canada at Massey College, to whom we have dedicated this book, provided inspiration and guidance.

Royal Progress: Canada's Monarchy in the Age of Disruption is the third in a series of books published for the Institute for the Study of the Crown in Canada by Dundurn Press in Toronto. The first, by Nathan Tidridge, was *The Queen at the Council Fire: The Treaty of Niagara, Reconciliation, and the Dignified Crown in Canada* (2015). Part one of the present volume provides a valuable sequel. The second book, a volume of essays entitled *The Canadian Kingdom: 150 Years of Constitutional Monarchy*, appeared in 2018 to mark the sesquicentennial of Confederation. Four among its authors have also contributed to *Royal Progress*.[2]

The Institute thanks Dundurn Press for its ongoing support of initiatives like these. It is indicative of their commitment to Canadian publishing that eight participants in the 2019 conference were also Dundurn authors, with books on display at the publisher's sales desk. Kirk Howard, founder of Dundurn and now publisher emeritus, was deservedly appointed a Member of the Order of Canada in 2018.

We acknowledge with much appreciation the invaluable assistance of the team at Dundurn Press, especially Kathryn Lane, associate publisher; Elena Radic, managing editor; Dominic Farrell, developmental editor; and Laura Boyle, art director. Our thanks also to Brian Lee Crowley, a contributor to the book, who suggested the title, and Senator Serge Joyal, another contributor, who provided the image for the cover.

Notes

1. Hon. James Bartleman, lieutenant governor of Ontario, 2002–2007; Hon. Judith Guichon, lieutenant governor of British Columbia, 2012–2018; and Hon. Henry N.R. Jackman, lieutenant governor of Ontario, 1991–1997.
2. Andrew Heard, D. Michael Jackson, Serge Joyal, and Nathan Tidridge.

INTRODUCTION:

THE CROWN IN A TIME
OF TRANSITION

D. Michael Jackson

Queen Elizabeth II is approaching a record-breaking seven decades as sovereign of Canada, the United Kingdom, and fourteen other Commonwealth realms. This book considers how the monarchy may evolve in Canada when her reign eventually comes to an end. Our contributors look at the historic relationship between the Indigenous Peoples and the Crown, the offices of the governor general and the lieutenant governors, the succession to the throne, and the likely shape of the reign of the next monarch. How will the venerable institution of constitutional monarchy adapt to changing circumstances in twenty-first-century Canada?

Royal Progress: Canada's Monarchy in the Age of Disruption is a deliberately paradoxical title. Can progress and disruption coexist? Certainly the third decade of the twenty-first century may be termed an age of disruption. Yet a theme running through the essays in this book is the continuity of the monarchical institution — its sheer staying power and adaptability, which have earned it the sobriquets of "shapeshifting Crown" and "chameleon Crown."[1] The authors of some of the essays recognize republican objections to the British-based constitutional monarchy in Canada. They respond by emphasizing two cardinal points: (1) the Canadian monarchy is here to stay for the foreseeable future because it is entrenched in the Constitution; and (2) the Canadian version of the Crown, if properly understood, supported, and adapted, is a distinct asset to Canada's political and social culture.

On this basis, the authors explore the positive roles the Canadian Crown can, does, and should fulfill, and changes that would facilitate the "progress" of the institution. These range from deepening and extending the link between the Crown and the Indigenous Peoples to thoroughly reforming the way viceregal representatives are chosen. Along the way, the authors offer specific proposals for strengthening the provincial dimension of the Crown, enhancing the relationship with the sovereign, and understanding the basic philosophy of constitutional monarchy. The final chapter, "Heritage and Innovation," neatly sums up the thrust of the book.

The Indigenous Dimension

In part one, "The Crown and Indigenous Peoples," four authors, two of them Indigenous, explore the meaning and potential of this centuries-old relationship. For them, it involves not just political and constitutional arrangements, but a profound, almost mystical, rapport with the sovereign, and with the principles and ideals she represents.

Respected Six Nations scholar Rick W. Hill Sr. and Nathan Tidridge, a perceptive observer of First Nations–Crown matters, hearken as far back as the seventeenth-century encounters of French and Dutch settlers with the First Nations in eastern North America. Negotiated through "wampum diplomacy," peace agreements between Indigenous nations and European monarchs allowed "radically different cultures to be incorporated into the complex networks and relationships that already existed between the various Indigenous nations." English, then British, settlers quickly picked up on the practice, which evolved into the rich and complex Crown-Indigenous rapport that continues to this day in Canada. For Hill and Tidridge, it is symbolized by the "Silver Covenant Chain of Peace," representing mutual respect and self-rule. This covenant chain protocol, they say, is not simply a colourful relic of the past: it is equally relevant today as an instrument to foster reconciliation. Of this, the historic gathering of Canadian viceregal representatives with Indigenous leaders in 2019 at the Chapel Royal of Massey College, Toronto, was a poignant illustration.

The leader who gave the keynote address at this gathering, National Chief Perry Bellegarde of the Assembly of First Nations, contributes the next chapter. He focuses on the history and intent of the treaties between the Crown and the First Nations. These constitute the "fundamental relationship, the foundation for this country called Canada. And that relationship was built on peaceful coexistence and mutual respect — to mutually share and benefit from these lands." Bellegarde emphasizes the essential role of the sovereign in the treaty process. While elected politicians come and go, the Crown is always there to symbolize and embody the principles and ideals of Canada's relationship with the Indigenous Peoples.

That relationship is not just one of governance or even peaceful coexistence, however. For Perry Bellegarde, the treaties are more than negotiated agreements: they are sacred covenants. "Our treaties are covenants with God, Creator, and all of creation." As Canadians face major challenges such as climate change and biodiversity, the First Nations can contribute the wisdom and experience of their world view to their non-Indigenous partners, developing with them a holistic vision of environmental stewardship. The national chief concludes that as "the direct representatives of the Queen and therefore the holders of a sacred trust on behalf of the Crown," the viceregal persons "are the caretakers and witnesses to this immutable relationship."

Appropriately, the third chapter in this part of the book is written by a former viceregal representative. Judith Guichon has spent much of her life close to the land: "I am at the core a farmer and an environmentalist." Perry Bellegarde's notion of the treaties as sacred covenants with the natural world therefore strikes a strong chord, and she notes that this view is shared by the Prince of Wales, heir to the throne. During her time as lieutenant governor of British Columbia, Guichon gave high priority to the provincial Crown's interaction with the First Nations, which, she affirms, needs to be characterized by "respect, relationships, and responsibility." She concurs with the authors of the preceding essays that the monarchy is key to the treaty relationship.

Indeed, Judith Guichon sees a parallel between monarchy and Indigenous culture: "Monarchs have a role somewhat like hereditary chiefs and elders in the First Nations communities. The monarch in our constitutional monarchy represents sober second thought and wisdom, not the next political cycle but rather enduring truths and the historical evolution of our nation through generations."

Reviewing and Reinvigorating the Viceregal Offices

The provincial manifestation of the Crown comes to the fore in the opening chapter of part two, "The Evolving Viceregal Offices." Fortuitously, its author is Andrew Heard, a prominent political scientist from Judith Guichon's home province, who has written about her use of the reserve power to refuse dissolution of the legislature in British Columbia in 2017.[2] This was in itself an illustration that viceregal powers are by no means obsolete: the lieutenant governors continue to fulfill the role of "guardians of the constitution, who may at times refuse to act on unconstitutional advice from their first ministers and cabinets."

The path of Canadian lieutenant governors toward the status of full representatives of the monarch, provincial equivalents of the governor general, has been long and circuitous and, in Heard's view, is still incomplete. At the time of Confederation the lieutenant governors were deemed not to be representatives of the Queen but merely federal officers appointed by and reporting officially to the governor general, but in reality reporting to the prime minister. Now they have come to embody a coordinate provincial Crown. But only to a point: Heard enumerates a number of instances, both symbolic and constitutional, where the lieutenant governors remain subordinate to the governor general. He offers some intriguing suggestions of how these anomalies could be overcome.

Regardless of their nominal status, the lieutenant governors are key figures in their jurisdictions, and not only in constitutional matters.

"Viceregal officers are supposed to personify the provincial society and polity as figures who are above politics and who can appeal to all in their community," says Heard.[3] He calls for a more effective way of selecting lieutenant governors, who must be politically neutral while in office. For better or worse, the appointment is entirely in the hands for the federal prime minister. When Conservative Stephen Harper occupied that position, he established a committee to advise on viceregal appointments. Despite its positive track record, his Liberal successor, Justin Trudeau, scrapped the process. For Andrew Heard, this reversion to political, sometimes overtly partisan, appointments, is regrettable.

In the next chapter, Senator Serge Joyal casts a critical eye on the appointment process for the *national* viceregal office. He looks at the impact of the personalities of the twelve Canadian governors general since 1952 "on the public perception of the sovereign and the role the Queen plays under our Constitution." Joyal sees a major change in these appointees. At first they came from a traditional background of public service and were familiar with the demands and expectations of the office. Starting in the 1980s, different career paths emerged. The four women appointees "had remained in the public eye during their careers, they were trusted figures in communications, and they were familiar television and media personalities."

For Joyal, this "celebrity status" is a two-edged sword: it gives the office of governor general a welcome public profile, but may have a negative impact on its constitutional functions. Another problem, especially when appointees are middle-aged rather than at the end of their careers, is what they do after their time in office and how that may be perceived by the public. A related issue is the term of office. Since the 1970s, prime ministers selecting the incumbents have adhered in most cases to a pattern of five-year mandates. This, points out Joyal, is the same as that of Parliament, less than that of some officers of Parliament, and much less than that of most prime ministers. Where then is the continuity supposedly embodied by the sovereign and the Crown? Senator Joyal deplores the diminution of the constitutional and ceremonial roles of the governor general, which only serves to enhance the already predominant power of the prime minister's office.[4]

The crux of the matter, then, is the prime ministerial grip on the appointment of the governor general, compounded by a recent trend to name people without appropriate background and experience. Joyal echoes Andrew Heard in calling for the reinstatement of the advisory committee on viceregal appointments pioneered by Stephen Harper. "Understanding the role of the person called upon to exercise the duties of governor general should be a prerequisite for selecting a candidate for the office," he concludes.

Given their relatively brief tenures, notes Senator Joyal, viceregal incumbents must rely heavily on the experience and knowledge of their staff and key advisors. In the following essay, journalist Dale Smith looks in this light at the historic position of secretary to the governor general. In the words of another writer, this person is expected to be a "confidant and chief of staff." [5] The role is complex and multi-faceted. If continuity in office is an issue for governors general, it is also, somewhat surprisingly, for their secretaries, despite the obvious need for institutional experience in the position. The long-standing practice of the secretary changing with each governor general was partially compensated for by drawing the appointees from "a pool of senior civil servants." Better still, in the 1960s to '80s and again in the 1990s, secretaries continued through the terms of several governors general, providing valuable corporate memory. Smith regrets the return to personal appointees of each governor general regardless of qualifications — in sharp contrast with the continuity found in the Queen's household.

Dale Smith deals with another senior appointment in his chapter: Canadian secretary to the Queen. This was not a position on the governor general's staff, deliberately so. Yet it had obvious links to Rideau Hall and provided a helpful complement. Starting in 1959, Canadian secretaries to the Queen were appointed on an ad hoc basis to coordinate royal tours, until the appointments became "indeterminate" in length in 1998. The position was made permanent by Prime Minister Harper in 2012 and located in the Privy Council Office, only to suffer the same fate as the viceregal appointments committee — discarded by Prime Minister Trudeau in 2015. This was an error, maintains Smith. The Canadian secretary to the Queen filled a number of valuable roles: coordinating royal tours with Rideau Hall, federal government departments, and the provinces and territories; organizing major celebrations like the Queen's Diamond Jubilee in 2012; arranging for members of the royal family to take on patronage positions with civil society organizations and the Canadian Forces; providing an ongoing, non-political, and informed link with Buckingham Palace. Most significantly, the Canadian secretary chaired the viceregal appointments advisory committee. Smith joins with Andrew Heard and Serge Joyal in urging a reinstatement, in the interest of a reinvigorated monarchy in Canada He applauds the belated appointment late in 2019 of a senior civil servant in the Privy Council Office to serve as Canadian secretary.

The Crown in Transition

Dale Smith emphasizes the importance of such measures in anticipation of the transition to the next monarch. The third part of *Royal Progress* addresses this very issue: "Moving Toward a New Reign."

The succession to the throne is of course the key to a new reign. To explain how this unfolds, Warren J. Newman examines history, conventions, and constitutional law. One thing is clear: on the death of a monarch, the heir immediately accedes to the throne. There is no interim. The coronation may follow some months later, but only affirms what has already taken place.[6] This may be evident for the United Kingdom, but what about Canada and the other Commonwealth realms? Here Newman guides us through more complex territory. Since the *Statute of Westminster* of 1931 and more specifically since the *Constitution Act, 1982*, British legislation does not apply to Canada. Yet the succession to the throne is defined in British law. How to square this apparent circle? Newman studies legislation, conventions, and precedents, such as the succession to the throne in 1936 on the abdication of King Edward VIII, to draw the conclusion that through the principle of "symmetry," Canada automatically recognizes as its sovereign the monarch of the United Kingdom identified in British statutes.[7] Yet according to a convention, the preamble to the *Statute of Westminster*, the realms (at the time called dominions) must approve changes to the British succession. Paradoxically then, while British law does not apply to the realms, the realms must approve a British law!

On this basis, Warren Newman robustly defends Canada's *Succession to the Throne Act, 2013*. It is, he says, supported "by sound legal principle but also by Canadian practice and tradition." The Act recognized legislation in the United Kingdom that eliminated male primogeniture in the succession and removed the bar to heirs to the throne marrying Roman Catholics. Objections by some scholars have centred on the presumed need to adopt a constitutional amendment in Canada, unanimously accepted by Parliament and all ten provincial legislatures. Citing eminent constitutional experts, Newman politely but firmly disagrees. Furthermore, he says, the 2013 legislation is "particularly well-adapted to the Canadian context" and "within the gamut of legal options ostensibly available ... the one that was clearly within the realm of the possible." This veiled reference to the perils of constitutional amendment suggests that the *Succession to the Throne Act, 2013* is a classic compromise, Canadian pragmatism at its best.

That pragmatism is the underlying theme of the essay by Brian Lee Crowley. Seeking to pinpoint why Canada fares well in its governance in comparison with other nations, notably the United States, he believes that it is "due in no small part to our continued embrace of monarchy and the institution of the Crown." He sees the difference between monarchies and republics as more fundamental than their respective constitutional arrangements: It is primarily what he calls "two different casts of mind." One — monarchical — is attached to tradition and experience; the other — republican — to rationalism and abstract principles.

Crowley uses the analogies of the gardener and the inventor to contrast these two casts of mind. The former is drawn to organic growth and pragmatic incrementalism. The latter seeks above all to follow logical first principles. For Crowley, the success of constitutional monarchy is due to its innate ability to adapt, to evolve, and — despite its lack of ideological underpinning — to work very well in practice for the people it serves. Not surprisingly, the "gardener" approach of unwritten tradition personified in the hereditary monarch appeals to the Indigenous Peoples, a point made in Crowley's essay.

Our final contributor, David Johnson, takes the bull by the horns, so to speak, with the title of his chapter: "Heritage and Innovation: The Future Reign of Charles III." Well aware that the succession to the throne will elicit "complaint and ridicule," even "scorn and anger," among republicans, he reminds us that the monarchy is "a natural default mode within the written Canadian Constitution." Given that reality, he considers how the next reign may differ from the present one and develop its own character, particularly in Canada. Johnson gives informed opinions on how the interests and proclivities and even passions of Charles, Prince of Wales, may colour his reign as King Charles III. Like his mother, he will be a promoter of the Commonwealth and of ecumenical and interfaith dialogue. He has an acute social conscience, which he has translated into action through influential charitable organizations. He is passionate about nature, ecology, environmental protection, and organic farming, all of which resonate with Canadians, particularly the Indigenous Peoples. Johnson, however, expresses concern that, given the ambivalence of much public opinion toward the monarchy and Charles himself in Canada, notably in Quebec, the Crown risks becoming an embarrassing anachronism rather than a vibrant Canadian institution.

Like Serge Joyal and Dale Smith, David Johnson wants to reinvigorate the Crown in Canada, and like them he has some specific proposals on how to do so. The new king and his family should immediately make themselves very visible through extensive tours and support important causes in their Canadian kingdom. Charles has created an arm of his leading charity, the Prince's Trust Canada, which is already a royal success story and should develop further. Johnson would particularly like to see a higher profile and more active role for the "viceregents" — the governor general and lieutenant governors — who do most of the Canadian Crown's work "on the ground." Their involvement in philanthropic endeavours and charitable causes should mirror that of the new monarch. He points to the Rideau Hall Foundation, established by former governor general David Johnston, as an example of what could be done to emulate the Prince's Trust Canada. The lieutenant governors, if not able to undertake similar endeavours in their provinces, could partner with these national initiatives, and with the "royals" themselves, to extend the reach and value and impact of the Canadian Crown throughout the land. It is a lofty goal, but David Johnson believes it is attainable.

In this introduction, the terms "paradox" and "pragmatism" have been used as descriptors of monarchy and particularly of its Canadian variant. The paradoxical nature of the Crown is evident. The institution is replete with seeming contradictions: constitutional authority, however, limited, vested in a hereditary sovereign reigning over a fully democratic, fully independent state; a monarch residing in the United Kingdom and identified under British law, yet accepted by Canada and other realms as their sovereign; viceregal representatives chosen by elected political authority and nonetheless, theoretically at least, superior to it; a mode of government dating back a millennium and still functioning in a twenty-first-century technological world, light years removed from its historical origins.[8]

The contributors to this volume appear comfortable with this paradox. A recurring theme in their essays is that, regardless of its theoretical deficiencies, the system works, and works well, thanks to its innate pragmatism — so in keeping with Canadian characteristics of tolerance, evolution, and practicality. Our authors, however, are not complacent about an institution they evidently treasure. They are apprehensive that the monarchy in Canada may decline into irrelevancy. They want to see instead a reinvigorated monarchy respected by Canadians and propose a series of imaginative but pragmatic and incremental measures to achieve this.

Those writing about the Indigenous relationship insist that this historic, fundamental dimension of the Canadian Crown must be taken more seriously, not less. It holds the key to true reconciliation and harmony with the First Peoples. The viceregal representatives can and should play a major part in this process. Their position and roles, whether constitutional, symbolic, or social, are crucial to the health of the monarchical institution in Canada. The profile and activity of the lieutenant governors can and should be reinforced to affirm the coordinate status of the provincial Crowns. But the method of appointing the "viceregents" and their senior staff is flawed and in need of review and reform. All three contributors addressing this issue deplore the elimination of the short-lived advisory process for national and provincial viceregal appointments and call for its reinstatement.

Ultimately, the term "vice" means acting as "substitute or deputy"[9] — in this case for the sovereign. If the institution of the Crown is to be authentic, the monarch cannot be relegated to a peripheral, token status. Attempts to portray the governor general as Canadian "head of state" are problematic in a federal monarchy.[10] Legal interpretations of the Crown as a constitutional abstraction risk depersonalizing a very human office.[11]

We see in part one of this book the symbolic importance attached to the person of the monarch by the Indigenous Peoples. The authors in part three emphasize this personal dimension. The succession to the throne focuses our attention on the next holder of an ancient yet contemporary position. In partnership with engaged viceregents, the future monarch's reign holds the promise of genuine renewal.

Yes, there can be royal progress in the age of disruption.

Notes

1. Cris Shore and David V. Williams, eds., *The Shapeshifting Crown: Locating the State in Postcolonial New Zealand, Australia, Canada and the UK* (Cambridge: Cambridge University Press, 2019); Anne Twomey, *The Chameleon Crown: The Queen and Her Australian Governors* (Sydney: Federation Press, 2006).

2. Andrew Heard, "British Columbia's 2017 Extraordinary Contribution to Constitutional Conventions," *Journal of Parliamentary and Political Law* 11 (2017).

3. See also Christopher McCreery, "The Provincial Crown: The Lieutenant Governor's Expanding Role," in *Canada and the Crown: Essays on Constitutional Monarchy*, ed. D. Michael Jackson and Philippe Lagassé (Montreal & Kingston: McGill-Queen's University Press, 2013).

4. For discussion of counterbalances to the concentration of power in the prime minister's office, see Serge Joyal, ed., *Protecting Canadian Democracy: The Senate You Never Knew* (Montreal & Kingston: McGill-Queen's University Press, 2003); and Serge Joyal, "The Crown and Prime Ministerial Government, or, The Slow Withering of the Monarchical Institution," in *The Evolving Canadian Crown*, ed. Jennifer Smith and D. Michael Jackson (Montreal & Kingston: McGill-Queen's University Press, 2012).

5. Christopher McCreery, "Confidant and Chief of Staff: The Governor's Secretary," in *Canada and the Crown: Essays on Constitutional Monarchy*.

6. See Ian Holloway, "The Law of the Succession and the Canadian Crown," in *Canada and the Crown: Essays on Constitutional Monarchy.*

7. See Robert E. Hawkins, "'The Monarch Is Dead; Long Live the Monarch': Canada's Assent to Amending the Rules of Succession," *Journal of Parliamentary and Political Law* 7, no. 3 (2013).

8. See D. Michael Jackson, "Political Paradox: The Lieutenant Governor in Saskatchewan," in *Saskatchewan Politics: Into the Twenty-First Century*, ed. Howard A. Leeson (Regina: Canadian Plains Research Center, University of Regina, 2001).

9. *The Canadian Oxford Dictionary*, 2nd ed. (2004), s.v. "vice-."

10. See D. Michael Jackson, *The Crown and Canadian Federalism* (Toronto: Dundurn, 2013), 225–35.

11. Serge Joyal, "The Oath of Allegiance: A New Perspective," in *The Canadian Kingdom: 150 Years of Constitutional Monarchy*, ed. D. Michael Jackson (Toronto: Dundurn, 2018).

PART ONE

THE CROWN AND INDIGENOUS PEOPLES

THE CROWN, THE CHAIN, AND PEACEBUILDING:

DIPLOMATIC TRADITIONS OF THE COVENANT CHAIN

Rick W. Hill and Nathan Tidridge

> We are Indians and don't wish to be transformed into white men. The English are our Brethren, but we never promised to become what they are.
>
> — Hodinohsó:ni response to request from New Light Reverend David Brainerd to build a church and offer weekly services, 1745[1]

Introduction

When Indigenous nations first encountered Europeans on Turtle Island (North America), they began incorporating them into their own long-established protocols of treaty making. Treaties created the necessary diplomatic space in which very different societies could attempt to communicate and negotiate complex relationships, despite radically different perspectives, including concepts of time and space. Rooted in centuries of ceremony and allegorical interpretation, the Crown was a natural vehicle for settlers to enter into long-term relationships with their Indigenous partners.

Treaties are not static creations, nor can they be captured by a written document. Interestingly, the words often used to explain a treaty can be interchanged with those used to describe the Crown: "honour," "enduring," "family," and "friendship." These words are necessarily abstract — their elasticity allows them to adjust to the fact that a treaty is meant to be constantly, and consensually, negotiated and interpreted. As well, understanding "treaty," like "Crown," requires oral interpretations and attention to story and ceremony, as well as a deep respect for the meanings behind the layers of protocol. Treaty, like the institution of the monarchy, is an organic creation that evolves — or devolves — depending on those who are engaged with it. Both treaty and Crown are meant to be the best reflections of their constituents.

This has not changed in the twenty-first century. The Queen and her representatives remain the "keepers of protocols" for non-Indigenous Canada — at the apex of our national and provincial ceremonies — and are rediscovering their roles as natural conduits into the treaty relationships that thread themselves across the land.

Establishing Treaties: The Two Row Wampum

Hodinohsó:ni ("People Who Make Longhouses") were one of the first Indigenous nations that made treaties with the Crown of England following the defeat of the Dutch colony of New Netherland in 1664 and the founding of the Province of New York. Together they established a treaty-making protocol, referred to as the Silver Covenant Chain of Friendship, that served to keep peace for nearly 150 years.

Originally a five-nation confederacy, after 1720 the Hodinohsó:ni included six nations.[2] The "Crown" meant the King or Queen of the United Kingdom,[3] but has come to mean the various governmental agencies and officials making agreements on behalf of the sovereign. This

2

involved, at various stages and to varying degrees, the Privy Council, the Lords of Trade, the Board of Trade and Plantations, Parliament, and the Colonial Office (1768–82), and the Home Office (after 1784). John A. Macdonald's *Indian Land Act* (1860) transferred "Indian Affairs" from the purview of the imperial government in London, displacing protocols that had been established through the Silver Covenant Chain, to colonial authorities in the Province of Canada. However, despite the erosion of the treaty relationships following Confederation and its successive legislation (the 1876 *Indian Act* being a prime example), the representatives of the sovereign as "Keepers of Protocol" are regularly entreated by their Hodinohsó:ni counterparts to return to the ancient protocols that bind them as kin.

Treaties are complex mediums, or relationships, that allow for nations to coexist and interact relatively peacefully. The reasons for making a treaty varied. Generally, a treaty council was required to

- renew peace and friendship between the parties,
- remove grief caused by murder or death,
- heal harm caused by treacherous settlers,
- compensate for lands taken illegally,
- halt rumours of war,
- compensate for harm caused by war,
- end unfair trade practices,
- end religious interference, and
- make up for unfulfilled promises from previous councils.

The Hodinohsó:ni had a well-established treaty-making procedure in place well before the English arrived in the seventeenth century. By making peace, the Hodinohsó:ni metaphorically extended the rafters of their bark-covered longhouses to their treaty partners, treating them like family, to live in peace under one roof (a common law). When the Dutch arrived on Turtle Island (North America), a treaty was needed that would allow radically different cultures to be incorporated into the complex networks and relationships that already existed between the various Indigenous nations. Around 1613 a treaty was entered into by the

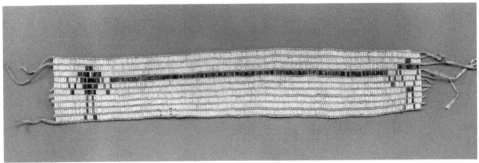

An early seventeenth-century representation in wampum of the Covenant Chain relationship, shown as a rope tying the Indigenous man (right) to the Dutch man (left).

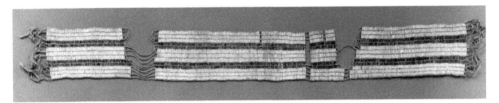

An original Aterihwihsón:sera Kaswénta, *or Two Row Wampum.*

Dutch and Hodinohsó:ni, codified in what is called the *Aterihwihsón:sera Kaswénta*, or the Two Row Wampum.

Wampum diplomacy employed strings or belts woven of wampum, which are small, tubular shell beads. Nothing was considered official unless it was accompanied with wampum. When an agreement or treaty was made, a special wampum usually codified its terms.

The treaty encoded into the *Aterihwihsón:sera Kaswénta* was archetypal: the Europeans were envisioned steering a large ship that contained their laws, beliefs, and traditions, which came alongside a Hodinohsó:ni canoe containing their laws, beliefs, and traditions. This treaty recognized the sovereignty of each partner, yet agreed on certain principles for sharing the waterways and this land.

Respecting Indigenous nationhood, the people of the ship would not try to steer the canoe, nor force the people of the canoe to abandon their laws, beliefs, and traditions. While history has shown how difficult it has been for the people of the ship to uphold their treaty pledges, the protocols for making amends were firmly in place. As well, there was a commitment that the treaty would last as long as the sun always made it bright on Earth, the waters flowed in a certain direction, and wild grasses grew green at a certain time of year. This would require periodic renewal of the agreements within the treaty so that subsequent generations would understand their obligations.

It was stated in the Two Row Wampum that in the days to come it might happen that dust would accumulate on the agreements, meaning that inattention to each other's needs might cause trouble. If that happened, it would be possible to wipe the dust from the agreements, making the relationship stronger. The treaty was understood to belong to the faces coming from deep underground (the future generations). Unfortunately, most people have become unaware of the nature and depth of relationships woven into the Two Row Wampum.

The oral descriptions and interpretations that come with wampum diplomacy are laden with analogies and metaphors. Language, and the metaphysical understandings that come with a specific vocabulary, are key to understanding the complex spaces inhabited by treaty, including the necessary protocols and ceremonies that are intrinsic to its very existence. It is within this realm that the Covenant Chain, called *Tehontatenentsonterontahkhwa* ("The thing by which they link arms" in the Mohawk language), comes into focus.

The Covenant Chain

On August 15, 1694, an Onondaga speaker stated to the representatives of the English Crown: "In the days of old when the Christians came first into this river we made a covenant with them first with the bark of a tree, afterwards it was renewed with a twisted withe, but in the process of time, least that should decay and rott the Covenant was fastened with a chain of iron which ever since has been called the Covenant Chain and the end of it was made fast at Onondaga which is the Center of the five Nations."[4]

By this the Onondaga speaker recalled the Two Row Wampum tradition established with the Dutch over eighty years earlier. The Hodinohsó:ni tied their canoe to the ship of the Dutch traders with a rope as a symbol of friendship and equality. The Dutch eventually replaced that rope with a sturdy iron chain, ensuring that the peaceful relationship would last for many generations in the future. However, they did not get to test the long-term strength of that chain, as New Netherland was invaded by the English in August 1664 and Dutch control of the colony was never restored. One of the first tasks of the new English administration was to make peace with the Hodinohsó:ni, who represented both a military and economic opportunity.

Assuming the treaty relationships honoured by the Dutch, English officials quickly embraced wampum diplomacy, while at the same time keeping meticulous written minutes of treaty councils, often reproduced on a large parchment with the terms written in English and signed by the principals who negotiated the treaty in the field.

In this way, three different methods of recording what took place at treaty councils now existed: oral, written, and wampum. While these methods of recording must coexist in order to properly capture a treaty, often times they did not agree, particularly concerning specific details. Indigenous nations relied upon the wampum and their oral memory of what took place, while the British favoured the written record.

The Covenant Chain was symbolic of the agreements that made the Hodinohsó:ni's relationship and friendship stronger with the Crown. The core idea of the Covenant Chain was that the Hodinohsó:ni, as well as other nations that joined later, and the Crown were linked in peace, having made solemn pledges to keep the principles of respect and friendship in the forefront of relationships that were meant to be enjoyed by all for many generations to come. The Covenant Chain symbolized that the parties would

- acknowledge one another as allies;
- inform each other about issues of concern;
- make amends for any transgressions that may have occurred on either side;
- ensure mutually beneficial trade;
- offer expressions of condolence for the losses suffered by either side;
- seek justice on a variety of political, economic, and social matters;
- renew peaceful relations;
- agree on a course of action that was mutually beneficial; and
- provide military assistance as needed.

A key cultural element in such a process was preparing the minds of the delegates to be able to earnestly speak from the heart, without confusion or deception. In order for a treaty council to have any chance of success, the parties had to first remove any lingering consternation from any trauma suffered by either party. This mind-spirit uplifting protocol began with the formation of the Great Law of Peace. Before the law, violence and death roamed the land. People's minds and spirits were wounded by what they experienced. Grief and sadness clouded their thinking. The future did not look bright.

In order for peace to prevail, the Great Law of Peace advocated that people use what is called the Good Mind, meaning they treat each other fairly and respectfully. To come to one mind on matters of peace, their minds had to be relieved of any fear, hurt, or prejudice. Wampum and empowering words were used to metaphorically remove the grief and sadness so that people's minds could once again experience love and hope. Both parties were expected to offer the powerful words shared in a metaphorical space called "the edge of the woods, near the thorny bushes."[5]

In looking at the Covenant Chain protocols between the English/ British Crown and the Hodinohsó:ni, it is important to realize that before the establishment of the Silver Covenant Chain with England in 1667, the Hodinohsó:ni had already created a treating protocol among Indigenous nations, which had been extended to the Dutch Republic and the French Crown in the sixteenth and seventeenth centuries. The customary practices, or protocols, employed in treaty making included the following:

1. Kindling the Council Fire — One party would call for the council and act as host by kindling the council fire over which the words would be shared. Fire was considered a purifier, requiring both sides to speak honestly and earnestly.
2. Wiping the Tears — One of the first orders of business was to console the invited party for any losses they may have suffered recently. Once consoled, the visiting party would offer the same ritual of condolence to remove the grief suffered due to the deaths of loved ones.
3. Hanging the Kettle — If war was to be declared, this was symbolized by the hanging of a kettle over the fire; if peace was declared, the kettle would be ceremonially removed from the fire.

4. Burying the Tomahawk — In the event that battles had taken place, the metaphorical tomahawk, a symbol of war, would be removed from the heads of the victims, cleaned, and buried to symbolize the recovery of normal relations.

5. Polishing the Chain of Friendship — A treaty council was called to address a specific list of issues, each codified by a specially designed wampum belt. When peace was first established with the Crown, a symbolic silver chain was created to represent the strength of the alliance. When trouble arose, it was represented by tarnish or rust on the chain that had to be removed (resolved). By agreeing on the peaceful resolution to the matters of concern, the treaty partners symbolically restored the silver chain to its original brightness. By polishing the chain, the parties renewed their commitment to one another.

6. Replanting the Tree of Peace — When the Hodinohsó:ni Confederacy was first formed, a tall white pine tree was planted to serve as a safe space where peace could be restored. When making peace, or reaffirming peaceful relations, the speaker would metaphorically replant the Tree of Peace, usually covering up the buried weapons of war.

7. Covering the Grave — When harm came to people, their deaths had to be acknowledged and atoned for, usually with presents of wampum or trade goods. This would placate the families of those who were killed, and the parties ceremonially covered their grave, placed a symbolic wampum belt over the grave, and pledged to never speak of the event again.

8. Smoking the Pipe of Peace — To conclude the council, after all of the wampum belts were passed back and forth, the delegates of both sides would smoke a pipe to acknowledge their concurrence with what had taken place. The smoke of the pipe carried their words up to the Spirit World, which was believed to be monitoring the treaty council progress.

9. Covering the Fire — At the conclusion of the treaty council, the embers of the council fire were covered over, to be rekindled in the future as needed.

Additional protocols, according to "Iroquois Treaty Speeches" by Cayuga Chief Jacob E. Thomas, recorded by Michael Foster, Museum of Civilization, 1976, included the following:

- The inviting council decides on the need for an invitation. It would require council approval. Invitation to be sent to the top authority, who then could decide on whom to send.
- Inviting council sends a runner: Messenger/Runner ("He is Hired") is delegated and sent with invitation wampum string ("His Burden") to invite the government to the council. An interpreter might also be assigned and a date set when the runners would leave.
- A message, such as to Polish the Friendship Belt or the Two Row Wampum, is put into a short string of wampum (the Burden). Notches (representing number of nights) would be made in an attached stick to keep track of time before the proposed council.
- Chiefs express their hopes that the runner stays healthy and is able to do his duty. The runner is given instructions on what to do when he arrives at the destination. He is to say that he is a messenger and will now tell what he was sent for, on behalf of the chiefs and the nations.
- Messengers would expect to be welcomed. The receiving nation would employ an interpreter. A welcoming speech is to be delivered. The receiving nations should offer the words of comfort, acknowledge the runners' long journey, offer a comfort seat, wipe away their tears, clean out their throat of dust from the long journey (offer drinking water), and clean their ears so they will hear clearly. Refresh the runners and assure that the Good Mind is present. A handshake offered at some point. "We are going to lead you to the comfortable 'mat' (seat) to listen to hear your words. You are free to stay as long as you want to stay."
- Runners of the inviting nation confirm what they have heard.
- The invitation message is delivered: "The leaders of the Hodinohsó:ni send their best greetings and regards to the leader, the people around him and the country itself. The council has appointed me to give you an invitation by this wampum. They would like you to be present (at a certain appointed time) to renew our treaties that were made with our ancestors."
- The receiving nation will confirm what they have heard.

- There is a tradition that after the runners have delivered their message, they will say that they are ready to go and get up as if to leave. However, the other side is to ask them to stay, as they have further things to say. The runners will agree to stay in order to deliver the entire message.
- The receiving nation asks for some private time to discuss the message. They will respectfully ask the runners to leave temporarily and say that they will call them back later in order to respond to the message. The runners will then retire to their lodging.
- The receiving nation meets to discuss the message and agree on a response and who will attend the proposed conference. They will call back the runners and deliver their formal response.
- Runners will depart and "push off their canoes."

The Covenant Chain as a Foundational Relationship

The Silver Covenant Chain of Peace, as perpetuated by the Crown, comprised several matters:

- First, it was a treaty relationship predicated upon the principles of mutual respect and recognition of the right of each government to self-rule.
- Second, it was a linking of arms, or holding of hands, symbolizing a firm commitment to uphold the terms of the treaty-based relationship.
- Third, it was a dispute-resolution mechanism, in which the parties agreed not to let any matter drive them apart.
- Fourth, it was represented by several wampum belts, usually with figures joining arms, or geometric figures with a central path that connects them together.
- Fifth, it was a three-link silver chain that represented an agreement to the Covenant principles: friendship, respect, and everlasting peace.
- Finally, it was also represented by a silver pipe with a small chain that attached the bowl to the stem; or a calumet, with eagle feathers attached to it.

A Mohawk speaker told colonial governor Sir Edmund Andros (1637–1714) in 1677 that because of their treaty relationship, they "are one, and one hart and one head, for the Covenant that is betwixt the Governor Generall and us is Inviolable yea so strong that if the very Thunder should break upon the Covenant Chain, it would not break it in Sunder." The governor responded: "Wee thank you that yea doe bury and forget all former discontents or Injuryes as wee doe the same, and never mor to be remembered, for wee know very well that our people have bein offensive to you."[6] Such platitudes were accompanied by special offerings, usually a wampum belt or a beaver skin. Purple and white wampum beads, woven into intricate designs, memorialized the pledges made on such occasions. The beaver hide symbolized the value of the trading alliance, and the dish with one spoon represented the sharing of the bounty of Mother Earth.

Onondaga Chief Sadeganaktie recalled the Covenant Chain as a foundational relationship with the colonists when he spoke to New York governor Fletcher in 1694:

> In the days of old when the Christians came first into this river we made a covenant with them first with the bark of a tree, afterwards it was renewed with a twisted withe, but in process of time, least that should decay and rott the Covenant was fastened with a chain of iron which ever since has been called the Covenant Chain and the end of it was made fast at Onnondage which is the Center of the five nations…. Since the time that the Governours have been here from the Great King of England we have made a Generall and more firme covenant which has grown stronger and stronger from time to time, and our neighbours seeing the advantage thereof came and put in their hands into the same chain, particularly they of New England, Connecticutt, New Jersey, Pensilvania, Maryland, and Virginia.
>
> But since that time that all Our neighbours have put in their hands into the covenant chain We have had great struggling and trouble from the Common enemy, the

french. Our Brother Cayenquiragoes wrist and Ours are tyred and stiff with holding fast the chain alone while the rest of Our neighbours sit still and smoake it. The Grease is melted from our flesh and drops upon our neighbours who are grown fatt and live at ease while we become lean. They flourish and we decrease ... The least Member cannot be touched, but the whole Body must feel and be sensible; if therefore an Enemy hurt the least part of the Covenant, we will join to destroy that Enemy, for we are one Head, one Flesh, and one Blood.[7]

When stressful or harmful incidents arose, the injured party was to "shake" its end of the chain to get the attention of the leaders of the other party. They would then gather, express condolences for the losses or harm done, make amends, and renew their commitments to each other. This process is referred to as polishing the chain — to renew it, make it strong, and give off the light of hope. The Crown has shaken its end of the chain many times, especially during the war with the Dutch, the French and Indian War, the American Revolutionary War, and the War of 1812, as well as the First and Second World Wars. The Hodinohsó:ni, who remained loyal to the Covenant Chain, always responded by sending warriors, supplies, and food.

The designs represent the Covenant Chain partners — the Hodinohsó:ni and the Crown. We can see one figure lower his war club as a gesture of peace. They hold the "path," which symbolizes their political connection as well as the pledge to keep the lines of communication open. The figure also represents the "fire" of each party — the political and spiritual authority of each nation to use the power of reason to end violence.

In 1754, Hodinohsó:ni speaker King Hendrick addressed the delegates at a treaty conference in Albany, both thanking and admonishing the British to keep the peace: "We thank you for renewing and brightening the covenant chain. We will take this belt to the Onondagas, where our council fire always burns, and keep it so securely that neither the thunderbolt nor the lightning shall break it. Strengthen yourselves and bring as many as you can into this covenant chain."[8]

The Extension of the Covenant Chain into the Great Lakes Region and Beyond

Thanks to the 1764 Treaty of Niagara, the Covenant Chain relationship and its incumbent protocols were extended into the Great Lakes region following the British victory over French forces during the French and Indian War (1754–63). The British Crown tried to consolidate its hold over North America by issuing the Royal Proclamation of 1763, but soon discovered, through events like Pontiac's War, that while the French had been defeated, their Indigenous allies had not. Separate negotiations employing Indigenous means of diplomacy would be required.

Representing King George III as superintendent of Indian Affairs, Sir William Johnson (1715–74) employed wampum diplomacy to convene a Great Council, encompassing some two thousand delegates representing twenty-four Indigenous nations, on the shores of the Niagara River near Fort Niagara in the summer of 1764. Johnson based himself at the fort, joined by most of the Hodinohsó:ni Nations,[9] while the Western Nations of the Great Lakes (not in treaty with the Crown) established themselves on the opposite bank, near present-day Fort George.

Johnson had had a long association with the Hodinohsó:ni since he first arrived in the Mohawk Valley in 1738 as an agent for the business interests of his uncle, Sir Peter Warren. His business dealings caused him to develop close relationships with the Mohawk and by 1745 he was appointed a colonel of the Six Nations. In 1755 Johnson was appointed superintendent of Indian Affairs (an appointment specifically linked to his relationship with the Hodinohsó:ni) and was fully immersed in the protocols associated with the Covenant Chain. It was around this time that he met Molly Brant (1735–96), a Mohawk clan mother. Through his common-law marriage with Molly, Johnson became brother-in-law to Joseph Brant (1743–1807), who would later become a captain in the British Indian Department.

By 1764 Johnson had become an authority in wampum diplomacy, which was also exercised by the Western Nations, and employed his expertise throughout the month-long negotiations at Niagara. The Covenant Chain provided a pre-existing framework for peaceful coexistence, and

Johnson worked to extend this relationship into lands surrounding the Great Lakes. Rather than develop a new construct, Johnson, as he later wrote to the British Lords of Trade, "thought it best to promise [the Western Nations], that they should be admitted into the Covenant Chain of Friendship."[10]

The Council of Niagara culminated on the morning of July 31, when Sir William Johnson crossed the Niagara River to meet with the assembled Indigenous dignitaries. Presenting them with two great wampum belts, Johnson declared: "Brothers of the Western Nations, Sachems, Chiefs and Warriors; You have now been here for several days, during which time we have frequently met to renew and Strengthen our Engagements and you have made so many Promises of your Friendship and Attachment to the English that there now remains for us only to exchange the great Belt of the Covenant Chain that we may not forget our mutual Engagements."[11]

As a versatile international treaty, the Covenant Chain now extended over much of the northern part of the continent, encompassing a multitude of nations and their relationships with the Crown. Its protocols evolved to meet the needs of a variety of different cultures, and endure to this day.

One hundred years after Johnson's Council at Niagara, the Prince of Wales (the future King Edward VII) visited Brantford, Ontario. Representing the Hodinohsó:ni, a nineteen-year-old Mohawk speaker named Oronhyatekha addressed the prince saying, "Although we have been separated from our Sovereign by the 'Great Water,' yet we have ever kept the chain of friendship bright, and it gives us joy to meet with the Heir Apparent to the Throne, that we may renew and strengthen that chain, which has existed between the Crown of England and the Six Nations for more than two hundred years."[12]

Conclusion: The Covenant Chain Today

The Hodinohsó:ni have been vigilant in informing each succeeding sovereign, and Canadian officials, of the Covenant Chain wampum agreement. Commemorating the three hundredth anniversary of a meeting between Mohawk representatives (erroneously recorded as "The Four Indian Kings") and Queen Anne in 1710, Queen Elizabeth II presented a set of silver handbells to the Mohawk Chapel in Brantford in 2010. The bells are engraved with the words, "The Silver Chain of Friendship 1710–2010."

When the Queen established her third chapel royal[13] in Canada in 2017, it was done using the Covenant Chain as a framework. The first two chapels had been established with Mohawk communities following the American Revolution (and are linked to an older chapel established by Queen Anne in the Mohawk Valley in 1711). The third chapel, established over two centuries later with the Mississaugas of the Credit (an Anishinaabe Nation), was rooted in the same relationship. Dedicated to the Treaty of Niagara, the Chapel Royal at Massey College displays near its altar a replica of the

Ontario lieutenant governor Elizabeth Dowdeswell poses at Massey College's Chapel Royal in 2018 beside a replica of the Covenant Chain Wampum exchanged at the Treaty of Niagara (1764).

Covenant Chain Wampum exchanged in 1764. As well, numerous pieces in the chapel evoke the Covenant Chain and the relationship it established.

On June 12, 2019, the governor general, lieutenant governors, and territorial commissioners of Canada gathered for A Council at the Chapel Royal. Sitting around a sacred fire, each viceregal representative presented a gift of Chapel Royal tobacco to Elder Garry Sault of the Mississaugas of the Credit. Following the welcoming ceremony, the dignitaries retired to the chapel itself to hear an address by National Chief Perry Bellegarde of the Assembly of First Nations. It was an example of a seventeenth-century treaty originally created with the Hodinohsó:ni providing a relevant mechanism and protocols of engagement in the twenty-first century. Lieutenant Governor Elizabeth Dowdeswell of Ontario observed this when she remarked in her address, "It was our predecessors who sat at the great Council Fires and other gatherings in what were the very first conversations between settlers and First Peoples. Here we have an opportunity to return to the principles that guided such interactions: talking, listening, sharing, and dreaming together."[14]

By a sacred fire at the Council at the Chapel Royal at Massey College, Governor General Julie Payette leads her viceregal colleagues in presenting Chapel Royal tobacco to Elder Garry Sault of the Mississaugas of the Credit.

The Covenant Chain protocol is not simply a colourful relic of the past. By agreement it was meant to last forever, as long as the sun rises, rivers flow, and grass turns green at a certain time of year. It is a great expression of hope that as long as the Earth lasts, our people will find ways to coexist and live in peace.

The time has come to reconsider what the Covenant Chain ethics and protocols might mean to facilitate true reconciliation in this country. This is the gift that our ancestors, as allies, passed on to us — the diplomatic tools to heal the wounds of the past, while keeping our eyes on the future, as we ensure that both Indigenous and settler peoples can thrive on this land through mutual respect, trust, and ongoing friendship.

Notes

1. Cited in James Axtell, *The European and the Indian: Essays in the Ethnohistory of Colonial North America* (New York: Oxford University Press, 1981), 78.
2. Another important confederacy in the region is the Three Fires Confederacy of Anishinabek Nations (Odawa, Potowatomi, and Ojibwa).
3. Since treaties during this period were being made between Indigenous nations and the English sovereign (the Kingdom of Great Britain would be established in 1707 and the United Kingdom in 1801), there is much debate within Indigenous communities concerning the legitimacy of a distinct "Canadian Crown" — a legal entity that emerged with the *Statute of Westminster* (1931) and without consultation with or the consent of treaty partners.
4. Cited in *The Papers of William Penn*, ed. Richard S. Dunn and Mary Maples Dunn, vol. 3, *1685–1700* (Philadelphia: University of Pennsylvania, 1987).
5. Hanni Woodbury, Reg Henry, and Harry Webster, "Concerning the League: The Iroquois League Tradition as Dictated in Onondaga by John Arthur Gibson," *International Journal of American Linguistics* 62, no. 1 (January 1996). On May 31, 2016, before formally meeting with the Mohawk Council of Akwesasne, the Hon. Elizabeth

Dowdeswell, lieutenant governor of Ontario, initiated an Edge of the Woods ceremony outside the Tri-District Elders Lodge.

6. L. Leder, ed., *The Livingston Indian Records, 1666–1723* (Mansfield: Pennsylvania Historical Association, 1956), 45–46.

7. Cited in Francis Jennings, ed., *The History and Culture of Iroquois Diplomacy: An Interdisciplinary Guide to the Treaties of the Six Nations and Their League* (Syracuse, NY: Syracuse University Press, 1995), 22.

8. Jeptha Root Simms, *History of Schoharie County, and the Border Wars of New York* (Albany: Munsell & Tanner, 1845), 126–29.

9. Some of the Senecas had allied with Pontiac and had attacked a British supply train. In a separate agreement at Niagara, Johnson pardoned the Seneca perpetrators in order to keep peace with the Hodinohsó:ni.

10. John Romeyn Brodhead, *Documents Relative to the Colonial History of the State of New-York: Procured in Holland, England, and France* (legislature), ed. John Romeyn Brodhead, 1814–73; Berthold Fernow, 1837–28 1908; E. B. O'Callaghan (Edmund Bailey), (Albany: Weed, Parsons), vol. 7, 648–50.

11. The wampum is described as "the great Covenant Chain, 23 Rows broad & the Year 1764 worked upon it, worth above 30 [pounds]." *The Papers of Sir William Johnson*, vol. 2 (Albany: University of the State of New York, 1953), 309–10.

12. Cited in J.R. (Jim) Miller, "The Aboriginal Peoples and the Crown," in *Canada and the Crown: Essays on Constitutional Monarchy*, ed. D. Michael Jackson and Philippe Lagassé (Montreal & Kingston: McGill-Queen's University Press, 2013), 261–62.

13. A chapel royal once referred to the clergy who accompanied monarchs during their travels across medieval England. In seventeenth-century England, chapels royal became associated with specific locations. Through settlement, chapels royal were planted in North America (Canada is the only Commonwealth realm outside of the United Kingdom to have them). All are in Ontario and all have an association with First Nations.

14. The Hon. Elizabeth Dowdeswell, "Lieutenant Governor's Remarks" (speech, The Indigenous Welcoming Ceremony, Massey College, Toronto, ON, June 12, 2019).

CROWN–FIRST NATIONS TREATY RELATIONSHIPS*

Perry Bellegarde

Introduction: Understanding the Treaties

Most of Canada is covered by treaties entered into between First Nations and the Crown. Both First Nations and British protocols and law were used in the treaty-making process. Treaties are foundational elements of the Crown–First Nations relationship and are greatly valued to this day. Treaties are international in character and affirm the sovereign status of First Nations as nations, and affirm that our sacred relationship to the land cannot be extinguished. Treaties are sacred commitments of peace, friendship, and mutual support that bind both sovereign parties. The treaty relationship is founded on immutable principles such as honour, trust, respect, justice, peace, friendship, sharing, and good faith. Violation of these principles violates the sacredness of treaties.

---

* This chapter is based on an address given by National Chief Perry Bellegarde of the Assembly of First Nations to Canada's viceregal representatives, gathered in the Chapel Royal at Massey College, Toronto, June 12, 2019. Wendy Moss Cornet provided the introduction.

At least seventy treaties were entered into between 1701 and 1923. These are sometimes called "historic" treaties or "pre-1974" treaties (to distinguish them from the land or self-government agreements entered into more recently). The pre-1974 treaties roughly fall into the following categories:

- Treaties of Peace and Neutrality (1701–60)
- Peace and Friendship Treaties (1725–79)
- Upper Canada Treaties and the Williams Treaties (1764–1862; 1923)
- Robinson Treaties and Douglas Treaties (1850–54)
- Numbered Treaties (1871–1921)

The famous 1701 Treaty of Montreal involved a peace treaty between First Nations and a representative of the King of France.[1] Our status as nations, our right to live as peoples in accordance with our own laws and ways, and the principle of consent were then affirmed by the British in the Royal Proclamation of 1763 issued by King George III. When the *Constitution Act, 1982* was enacted, treaty rights were affirmed and recognized along with First Nations inherent rights and title (section 35). The Supreme Court of Canada has acknowledged Crown–First Nations treaties as sacred. In speaking of Treaty No. 8, for example, the court stated:

> It is an agreement whose nature is sacred. See *R. v. Sioui*, [1990] 1 S.C.R. 1025, at p. 1063; *Simon v. The Queen*, [1985] 2 S.C.R. 387, at p. 401. Second, the honour of the Crown is always at stake in its dealing with Indian people. Interpretations of treaties and statutory provisions which have an impact upon treaty or aboriginal rights must be approached in a manner which maintains the integrity of the Crown.[2]

In a 2018 case, an Ontario court examining the Robinson-Huron treaties of 1850 found that "the honour of the Crown requires that the Crown fulfil their treaty promises with honour, diligence, and integrity."[3] The same court stated: "The process by which the terms of the Royal

Proclamation of 1763 … would be implemented reflected Crown recognition of Anishinaabe sovereignty that survived the unilateral declaration of Crown sovereignty."

Treaties touch every institution of government in Canada that is connected to the Crown. This includes the executive, the legislature, and the judiciary, as well as the Queen's representatives in Canada, the lieutenant governors and the governor general. The treaty commissioners who negotiated treaties on behalf of the Crown explicitly presented themselves as direct representatives of the Crown. The oral history that forms part of First Nations law is an integral part of treaty. Oral history is clear that there was no surrender of land. The Queen's representatives in their opening remarks for Treaty No. 4, for example, stated: "What I offer you, will never take away your style of life. It is on top of what you already have." Through the treaty commissioner, the Queen also promised to maintain a commission through which her promises would be delivered justly, according to the treaty, with the utmost exactness.

There is no treaty commissioner office today. However, the lieutenant governors and the governor general of Canada are the direct representatives of the Queen and therefore the holders of this sacred trust on behalf of the Crown. Each of these office holders must be aware of this history and the significance of treaty as part of their office. While the government of the day has a role to operationalize the treaty obligations held by the Crown, the Queen's representatives are the caretakers and witnesses to this immutable relationship. The Crown–First Nations treaty relationship is not founded in colonialism or in rights denial, but rather the equality and sovereignty of peoples and our agreement to share the land without dominating one another. A proper understanding of treaties is tied to many important issues respecting treaty implementation.

First Nations often say that the treaty relationship is above policy and above federal and provincial law. That is difficult for some to understand, but the reason for this is quite simple — treaty and treaty relationships came first; and this country exists as it does only because of treaty relationships. Treaties between the British Crown and First Nations are what made the Canadian Constitution possible. The United Nations Declaration on the Rights of Indigenous Peoples affirms the international status of Indigenous Peoples, including our status as peoples holding the right to self-determination. The Declaration does not create new rights. Rather, it affirms rights that are inherent to us as peoples. The Declaration is grounded in the universality of all human rights. Article 37 speaks to treaty relationships and states that

> Indigenous peoples have the right to the recognition, observance and enforcement of treaties, agreements and other constructive arrangements concluded with States or their successors, and to have States honour and respect such treaties, agreements and other constructive arrangements.

We are now in a period of restoring a proper understanding of the nature of the treaty relationship between the Crown and First Nations — one that is more fitting with respect to the original protocols as well as one more consistent with international law, including international human rights law.

National Chief Perry Bellegarde addresses Canada's viceregal representatives in the Chapel Royal at Massey College, Toronto, June 2019. Seated on the left are Governor General Julie Payette, Ontario Lieutenant Governor Elizabeth Dowdeswell, and Quebec Lieutenant Governor J. Michel Doyon.

Interpreting the Treaties Today

I wish to share not only my understanding of our special treaty relationship with the Crown but to also share my vision of what reconciliation really means. For First Nations people, everything begins with the lands. The lands and waters sustain all of us. So I will focus on the situation of our natural world and the role of First Nations peoples in meeting the environmental challenges facing all nations.

Elected leaders come and go. During their tenure, we want them to focus on making the transformational changes we all want and need. The role of the viceregal representatives of Her Majesty Queen Elizabeth II, whose reign has spanned twelve prime ministers, allows them to promote a sense of identity. Bound by our collective beliefs in reconciliation, what could that identity be and become? With the promise of peace, friendship, mutual support, and respect, if we fulfilled the promise of our treaties together, think how enriched and mature the Canadian identity would become in this twenty-first century.

Our ancestors entered into treaties in the spirit of peaceful coexistence and mutual respect. The challenges now faced by First Nations people were never meant to be; the treaty relationship says otherwise. There is a huge gap in the quality of life between First Nations and Canadians. The federal government's Community Well-Being Index shows that the gap has not changed at all since 1981.

This Covenant was created through ceremony — the use of the pipe and the sweat lodge. What we have done through ceremony, we cannot break. And that is why there is sacredness to this treaty. That is why we have songs about the Queen, and about the Crown. That is why we will always maintain this, because this is our truth. These are our teachings. Our treaties are covenants, with all of creation.

The treaty relationship is that fundamental relationship, the foundation for this country called Canada. And that relationship was built on peaceful coexistence and mutual respect — to mutually share and benefit from these lands. The treaty medallion I often wear says it all. On one side of the medallion you see the non-Indigenous man shaking hands with the Indigenous man — and you see the hatchet is buried at their feet, symbolizing peace. You see the sun and the water and the grass. As long as the sun shines, the waters flow, and the grass grows, this Covenant will remain in effect. You see the big tipis and then the smaller ones representing the future, representing generations now and those yet unborn.

On the back of the treaty medallion you see Queen Victoria. Our leaders entered into treaties with Great Britain, so this treaty medallion says it all and speaks to our relationship and this very important symbol. Nations make treaties. Treaties do not make nations. The right to self-determination is our most fundamental right. We have our lands, our laws, our languages, our own peoples, and our own identifiable forms of government. The inherent right to self-determination is recognized with those five elements. We exercised that right and entered into treaties with the Crown. We used that right to self-determination. And so we maintain this treaty relationship with the Crown — the sacred commitments each side made as sovereign nations to mutually support one another.

You need three things to understand the treaties.

First, the treaties themselves. There are two ways to interpret the treaty — the spirit and intent drawn from the oral record from our law, versus the written English words typically sent back by bureaucrats afterwards. These words did not match the actual oral treaty exchange and protocol, nor the understanding of First Nations parties.

So, for example, Treaty 6 says that a medicine chest will be kept at the house of the Indian Agent and in times of sickness and famine we will be looked after. What is the spirit and intent behind that clause? We believe that this is the spirit and intent for health care. And what does it mean when it says, when you are ready to settle down on your reserve we will provide a little red brick schoolhouse and teach your children the cunning of the white man? What does that mean? A little red brick schoolhouse? Or an education from kindergarten to Grade 12 through to post-secondary institutions such as university? That is the spirit and intent of education. And then our hunting, fishing, and trapping rights were guaranteed to continue our way of life and connection to the land. Those are the essence of the spirit and intent versus the legalistic interpretation. The spirit and intent of the treaties reflects our understanding — the First Nations understanding — of the treaties.

I do not understand what "cede, surrender, and relinquish" means. But I understand sharing. I understand living a life together as family. And those are the terms that are used. So we need that spirit and intent interpretation to be written down. We also need Alexander Morris's treaty book, while keeping in mind it does not represent the whole of the treaties. He was the Queen's commissioner put in place to negotiate these international treaties with First Nations. He wrote about it in his book, *The Treaties of Canada with the Indians of Manitoba and the North-West Territories*, first published in 1880.[4] And, most importantly, we need the elders' history and interpretation of the treaty, their understanding as conveyed orally.

With those three things, we will have an understanding of the treaties, our relationship with the Crown, and why we have that strong connection to the treaties. We see the treaty relationship as the way we must conduct ourselves at all times; in that spirit of partnership, sharing, and mutual respect.

I have experienced the potlatch in Alert Bay with the Kwak'wak'wakw peoples and their guests, other coastal peoples; the Nuu-chah-nulth, the Heiltsuk, the Squamish, the Musqueam, the Nuxalk, the Tsimshian, the Tlingit, the Haida, and many more. And what an experience as the ancient stories are sung and brought to life with masks and blankets! All at once we are connected in the present to our past, and to who we are. It is powerful. And I see the similarities of the ceremonies from the West Coast, to those of the Dene in the North, to the Anishinaabe more centrally, to the East Coast Mi'kmaq, to my own, the Sun Dance of the prairies.

The privilege to help and learn from our old people for more than thirty years remains with me. Together, every year, we build the Sun Dance lodge with the old men and old women telling us what to do in their sometimes fun and cheeky ways. With our four-day fast, year after year, with the singing of our songs, with the coming-together year after year in prayer with our friends and families and our old ones in the spirit world, we invoke all of creation, give thanks, and pray for many things.

And what matters more is that we see ourselves in each other: as leaders who have set out to make the dreams of our old people real and to move through this struggle with our unwavering desire to improve the lives of our peoples. Each and every one of us here can and must continue to make a difference.

First Nations and the Environment

The numbered treaties — Treaties 1 to 11 — were consecrated when our ancestors called upon all of the grandmothers and grandfathers to witness their Covenant with the Crown. So, Grandfather Sun was called upon to witness that Covenant; the Water Spirits were called upon to witness that Covenant. Mother Earth was called upon. As long as the sun shines, the rivers flow, and the grass grows this Covenant will remain in effect for generations now and for those as yet unborn.

The challenges now faced by all of us with the rapidly declining state of our natural world were not meant to be.

First, climate change: we must ensure that the Earth does not warm more than 1.5 degrees. And second, biodiversity: human actions threaten more species with global extinction now than ever before. Around one million species face extinction unless action is taken. Plastic pollution has increased tenfold since 1980 and is entering almost every living creature, including human beings. The treaty relationship says this was not meant to be.

That is the link to the climate and biodiversity crisis now staring humanity in the face. We consecrated these international treaties with the Crown in the presence of all of creation, and now we use our world view to show you why the present state of our natural world — the climate crisis, the threats to biodiversity — must be addressed with our collective wisdom and knowledge.

First Nations world views see and understand all of creation as a family. And that is the link — with Father Sky, Mother Earth, Grandfather Sun, Grandmother Moon, and all the spiritual guardians having witnessed those covenants. That is why we say that sacredness, that sanctity of agreement, that sanctity of contract, is above all else. Our treaties are covenants with God, Creator, and all of creation. That is why these treaties are so special. That is why the covenant cannot be broken by mankind. That is why this relationship with the Crown is so important.

We are all joined by our natural world. All my friends, my relatives. We are "the two-leggeds." And it does not matter if you are black, white, yellow, or red. We are the two-legged tribe. Every day we give thanks to Grandfather Sun, our Grandmother Moon, to the Star People, to Father Sky and Mother Earth, the ones who fly, the ones who crawl, and the ones who swim. We give thanks to the four-leggeds. And we acknowledge the Grandmothers who look after the water — the salt water, the fresh water, rain water, and the water that comes with new life. We, as First Nations, are joined by our creation stories and our common values as First Nations people with our different spirit beings such as Kluskap, Nanabozho, Weesageechak, Napi, Coyote, Raven, Inktoom, and more. We learn teachings of who we are, where we are from, and our spiritual connections to our lands. When our ancestors entered into treaties, this is what they invoked and what they wanted to preserve.

Bound by a collective commitment to realize the promises of the treaties, what could the identity of Canada be and become? First Nations are uniquely positioned to lead efforts to protect, conserve, and sustainably manage the environment and biodiversity. We are ready to share our knowledge and contribute as peoples and as equal members in this treaty relationship and the human family. We must work together to develop a vision of environmental stewardship that is global and holistic, and that takes us beyond existing targets and timelines, toward a sustainable future for all generations.

Canada, I believe, must increase and accelerate our contributions and leadership to meet the United Nations Sustainable Development Goals, to decarbonization, to biodiversity, and to conservation. It is time for Canada to support not only a right to development but the right to sustainable development, at home and in UN General Assembly resolutions.

Around the world, we can already see the destabilizing impacts on economies, individual well-being, and human security of climate change impacts: loss of habitat, biodiversity, Indigenous Peoples' traditional foods, and further loss of food security, flooding, rising sea levels, extreme weather events, and plastics turning up in every living being including ourselves. Children around the world are telling us, the leaders of this generation, that they are unhappy, and insist that we at least meet the modest goals we have already set for ourselves. What does that say about us, when our children are taking on our worries and having to remind us of our responsibilities? Clearly, we must do better to avoid and mitigate increased climate change impacts. We will be abdicating our responsibilities to future generations and to the Earth unless we meet that challenge.

First Nations peoples need greater involvement in the development of solutions. And First Nations people must have the strength and health and *place* to be part of this. We were to mutually share and benefit from these lands. While we must continue to be intent on eradicating poverty and improving the well-being of all, we must actually execute effective plans and strategies for upholding our duties to care for our mother, the Earth, and all that she holds. We must be able to turn on the tap and drink the water in our homes. We must be able to raise our own children and grand-children. We must watch with pride as our young people graduate. We must listen with joy as our people talk and sing in our languages. We must know that women, children, and young people live free from the threat of violence and feel safe and secure.

Conclusion

We must have the Canada that sees our knowledge-keepers deliver all that our ancestors taught us safely into the hands of our young people. We must teach people about our inherent and treaty rights and the importance of self-determination. And we must inspire our young people to take pride in the languages and traditions sacred to First Nations people. Only then can they accept with passion and commitment their responsibility as stewards of both our lands and the teachings and traditions of our ancestors. Our young people are the true beneficiaries of the wealth and riches of these lands. It will all pass one day into their hands for them to hold until they pass it on to future generations. Only by our example will they learn how to be strong guardians and wise stewards.

As the direct representatives of the Queen and therefore the holders of a sacred trust on behalf of the Crown, viceregal persons must be aware of this history and the significance of Treaty as part of their high office. While the government of the day has a role to operationalize the treaty obligations held by the Crown, the Queen's representatives are the caretakers and witnesses to this immutable relationship. Properly understood, the treaty relationship is not founded in rights denial or a colonial mentality but, rather, in the equality and sovereignty of peoples and our agreement to share the land without dominating one another.

This could be what Canada is and becomes.

Notes

1. The Mik'maq entered into a concordat in 1601 with the Vatican (a concordat is essentially an agreement only entered into by the Vatican and the pope with sovereign nations).
2. *R. v. Badger*, [1996] 1 S.C.R. 771.
3. *Restoule v. Canada (Attorney General)*, [2018] ONSC 7701.
4. Alexander Morris, *The Treaties of Canada with the Indians* (Toronto: Belfords, Clarke, 1880; Saskatoon: Fifth House, 1991).

A Matter of Respect:

Crown-Indigenous Relations
in British Columbia

Judith Guichon

I f not a constitutional monarchy, then what, exactly, would Canada be? Without the symbols of the Canadian Crown, our red maple leaf, and our national anthem, which connect us from coast to coast to coast, would we stand as tall? Would we be this distinctive, inclusive, open, and civil society that so many are anxious to join if Canada were a republic? Who or what would stand between First Nations and complete homogenization by short-term political ambition? In 2019, we celebrated the fifty-fourth anniversary of our flag. This red maple leaf is a symbol of our unity as a nation from sea to sea to sea and represents all the citizens of Canada, no matter our race, our language, our culture, our religion, or our beliefs.

While I was in Prince Edward Island in my previous role as lieutenant governor of British Columbia, we stood in the footsteps of the Fathers of Confederation and it struck me that ours is a nation born through conversation, not confrontation, and it is this ongoing discussion that allows us to evolve, to accommodate, and to be inclusive. Have we made mistakes? Absolutely. But I believe that we continue to learn from, and try in good conscience to repair those errors and to grow, not in territory but in stature and in magnanimity. Indigenous nations have long histories of honouring regalia, ceremony, and symbols, which are all important parts of their stories as well.

At the bottom of my coat of arms are what I refer to as my three *R*s. Not reading, writing, and arithmetic but rather *respect, relationships,* and *responsibility,* because I believe that in this life we must all have respectful relationships with one another *and* with the land that supports us, and that we have a responsibility to leave our place on this Earth better for all those who will come after.

As a rancher, I have lived for years in relative isolation and have welcomed visitors as they bring news and innovative ideas, and add variety and excitement to our daily lives. When newcomers first arrived on the shores of North America, they, too, were welcomed as guests. This warm greeting set the tone and led to co-operation between the Indigenous residents and the newcomers. Many explorers survived because of the knowledge they gained from local First Nations. Problems developed when the guests stopped acting like visitors and failed to *respect* the hospitality, the civility, and the customs of their hosts. Some newcomers assumed that they were more experienced, and had more sophisticated governance, art, language, and possessions. This perceived superiority and pressure from the homeland led them to assert dominion over the Indigenous residents. Unfortunately, the nature of colonization is to overrun and supplant existing norms in the search for new resources. This story is not unique to Canada and continues to be repeated around the world today. In addition, there were individual Indigenous citizens who also benefitted inordinately by making accommodations.

Humans, as they urbanize, tend to lose connection with and respect for all the life-giving services provided by the land. This lack of respect is reflected in many ways, including a loss of understanding of the stabilizing influence of natural cycles, and deterioration of interactions between humans. As cities grow, often the layers of concrete that separate us from nature and from one another also increase. Unfortunately, this human frailty is only too well recorded in Ronald Wright's *A Short History of Progress*. "Civilizations have developed many techniques for making the earth produce more food — some sustainable, others not. The lesson I read in the past is that the health of land and water ... can be the only lasting basis for any civilization's survival and success."[1]

In a collection of selected speeches of Marcus Tullius Cicero, the very first section in "How to Run a Country" talks about natural law being the foundation on which government should be built. From the surviving passages of his book *On the State*, I quote:

> True law is a harmony of right reasoning and nature. It applies to everyone in all places and times, for it is unchanging and everlasting. It commands each of us to do our duty and forbids us from doing wrong. Its commands and prohibitions guide good and prudent people, but those who are wicked will listen to neither. It is not right to try to alter this law. We cannot repeal any part of it, much less do away with it altogether. No senate or assembly of the people can free us from its obligations. We do not need anyone to explain or interpret it for us. ... It applies to all people everywhere — past, present, and future.[2]

The Haida Nation, when carefully articulating their constitution for the first time in 2003, stated, in part: "Our Culture, our heritage, is the child of *respect* and intimacy with the land and sea" (my emphasis). Again, we see that most important word, "respect"! It strikes me that, although separated by several thousand years and thousands of miles of land, we see a very similar philosophy in these governance models.

I was born in Montreal, but fortunately my father bought a farm in eastern Ontario where I spent every weekend, summers, and all holidays. I had the best of both worlds, with the Montreal Canadiens all week and cows on the weekend! I knew my way around the urban landscape but had also felt the rich tilth of soil beneath my feet. Unfortunately, growing up in Montreal in the 1950s and '60s, if we saw *either* a "cowboy" or an "Indian," we knew there was a movie being filmed in town. Although Montreal has many First Nations living within its greater area, I knew absolutely nothing about any of my Indigenous neighbours or our early history in Canada. There is a terrible vacuum in the understanding of our past. This is finally changing and Canadians are beginning to learn our history. It is absolutely paramount that we open the cracks and explore the stories. Canadians must become comfortable in their own skin.

After travelling across Canada to Whitehorse some fifty years ago, I was fortunate to meet and marry a rancher and we returned to the family ranch in the interior of British Columbia. Our neighbours are the people on an Upper Nicola Indian Reserve, part of the Okanagan Nation. Even though I now had the opportunity to work with and become friends with many of our neighbours, I still knew very little about residential schools, the *Indian Act*, the inability of Indigenous people to vote even when many had fought for this country in the two great wars. Like so many Canadians I remained abysmally ignorant.

When I was offered the position of lieutenant governor, I consulted only one friend outside of family, a retired chief of the Upper Nicola Band. Did he feel I could accomplish anything useful? He urged me to go ahead. Now my education began in earnest. I well remember a talk by Shawn Atleo, who advised that Canadians needed to *own* their own history. I was also privileged to hear Douglas White lecture on the early legal battles fought by his ancestors. I spent time with Louise Mandell, chancellor of Vancouver Island University, whose legal battles in our courts have helped carve new roads for First Nations. I was also a witness at the Vancouver reconciliation events and was absolutely amazed by some of the horrific stories, related with such dignity. I was privileged to visit the legislature of the Nisga'a Nation, where they are reintroducing their values, philosophies, and spirituality into the laws that govern their community. Perhaps my favourite yearly ceremony was the First Nations Remembrance Day Service in downtown Vancouver, held November 8, where Indigenous and Asian veterans gathered, representatives of the diverse collection of Canadians who fought so valiantly for this land that they all love.

When I read Cicero's section on natural law, it reminded me of First Nations philosophy and their traditional hereditary decision making. If you believe that your great-great-great-grandchildren are going to inherit "this Place," it is reflected in your stewardship of the land. The band councils system, the construct of government under the *Indian Act*, is a municipal-style system designed to extinguish traditional hereditary power and decision making. These band council rules have little or no relationship to Indigenous beliefs or clan systems. They were given onerous, complex responsibilities to deliver all services to their community including municipal, social, recreational, educational, and health services, with limited funding or training.

Traditionally, First Nations carried on their business based on consensus. Hereditary chiefs were trained from an early age and had to earn the respect of the members of their community. This model of leadership required chiefs to be mediators rather than dictators, and to guide the community members to cooperatively make decisions. Elders have always been held in high esteem by members of First Nations bands. They are teachers, historians, judges, ecologists, and storytellers. Their advice was listened to and respected.

As we look around the world, we see a similar philosophy reflected in monarchs. They also do not fill their role for a short-term elected reign, but rather for an inherited duration often measured in decades. Most monarchs are prepared from birth to fulfill these duties. Their vision of the future encompasses generations and the realization that the conditions left when they end their reign will be inherited by family. They have a role somewhat like hereditary chiefs and elders in the First Nations communities. The monarch in our constitutional monarchy represents sober second thought and wisdom; not the next political cycle but rather enduring truths and the historical evolution of our nation through generations.

In Canada, the monarch presently is the ultimate guardian of our parliamentary democracy and of our civility. In 2005, when addressing citizens in Edmonton, Her Majesty Queen Elizabeth II said, "Your enduring ties to the Crown stand not only for a respect for heritage but also for the principles of peace, order, and good government developed by the Fathers of Confederation, who envisaged and worked so diligently to make this country a reality." The Honourable Henry Jackman, former lieutenant governor of Ontario, said it so well: "For the Monarchy is much more than a person.

It embodies the constitutional framework of our freedoms, the set of beliefs and attitudes of tolerance that make up this great country and make it distinctive. The Queen is the symbol of what we are today and the history of which we are the result, and which is part of us."

As democracy has evolved over the last seven hundred years, power has gradually been distributed more broadly among citizens. Again, Cicero speaks about the balance of power and his vision of ideal government: "A moderate and balanced form of government combining all three is even better than kingship. This sort of state would have an executive with pre-eminent and royal qualities, but also grant certain powers both to leading citizens and to the people according to their wishes and judgment.... While a single form of government often turns into something else, a mixed and balanced system remains stable."

Canada is such a vast and unwieldy physical land mass. We are diverse in nature both physically and culturally. Having lived in two territories and three provinces, I can attest to this personally. The morning commute to work in Whitehorse, Yukon, is very different from that in Montreal. But our ties and our history, like that of a family, have allowed the provinces and territories to evolve independently and to survive family squabbles, including horrors such as the residential schools, the battles of Louis Riel, the Fenian Raids, and the fight for independence in Quebec with the rise of the FLQ, just to name a few. Through all these upheavals, all of us, including First Nations, have looked to the Crown for steadfast encouragement, ongoing respect, and for a relationship that is so much more than political. It is for this symbol of wisdom, of stability, and of democratic principles and durability that we turn to the Crown.

We are now far more aware of the very grave wrongs done in the past, and finally school curricula are being updated to include realistic history. We have found many upon whom to lay the blame. We like to say that it was the church, or the government who imposed the unjust laws, but of course, the government is us and only acts with our licence. Gradually, we are learning about the complicity of citizens across Canada in the attempt to assimilate the Indigenous people and their lands.

Churches certainly bear responsibility, but there are also many stories of individuals within religious organization who acted solely out of love rather than greed or fear. Such a story is that of the first Sisters of St. Anne who ventured west. Three very young French girls left Vaudreuil, Quebec, and made the arduous journey to Victoria, where they found a small log building with a dirt floor, no well, and no amenities. They came to teach whoever showed up and to care for the sick and dying. What courage those young women demonstrated. This order went on to found schools, hospitals, and nursing schools. As always, there are stories both of tremendous courage and of terrible betrayal and we must be careful when we generalize.

During my tenure as lieutenant governor, we had several royal visitors. While entertaining Prince William and Kate, Duke and Duchess of Cambridge, we were very privileged to display the *Witness Blanket* created by First Nations artist Carey Newman. Carey is of British, Kwagiulth, and Salish heritage. The *Witness Blanket* is a wooden-framed structure some seven feet tall and is made in sections that fold, representing a blanket, a comfort to all. Artifacts were collected from residential schools right across Canada to create this incredible exhibit. It is a story that we can witness, acknowledge, and soak up. We honour the children and all their families who suffered through those atrocities. It is hard, but it is a necessary part of the healing and must take place so we can move on as one nation. Gradually, we are learning and will forgive and be forgiven. The *Witness Blanket* gives us vocabulary to understand the past and is an opportunity to rekindle the council fire where we can come together to foster a healthy future for all our children and grandchildren. This work of art is the product of love and therefore is not threatening. It is an appropriate teaching tool that allows our royal family and all Canadians to accept the truth about our history and to begin to build bridges on the long progress toward reconciliation.

The United Nations Declaration on the Rights of Indigenous Peoples as adopted in 2007 offers guidance on co-operative relationships with Indigenous Peoples to states, the United Nations, and other international organizations. Canada endorsed the Declaration with a statement of support in 2010. This was a commitment to continue working in partnership with Indigenous people in creating a better Canada. And then, in 2016, Canada officially adopted the Declaration without qualification. This adoption was heralded by First Nations leaders such as Cree lawyer Chief Wilton Littlechild. The former commissioner of the Truth and

Reconciliation Commission called it "a step forward in the long process of 'harmonizing' Canada's Laws with standards set in the declaration and in improving relationships." Chief Littlechild said, "Today would not be too late to start the journey together."

This Declaration will create challenges for every level of governance, and many are nervous about the implications on land issues. But in Canada as it unfolds, it will build on the Royal Proclamation of 1763 and the Treaty of Niagara of 1764, which reaffirm the "nation-to-nation relationship between Aboriginal peoples and the Crown." The progress with UNDRIP, as it has become known, will not require extensive changes to law, as Indigenous and treaty rights are already protected in Canada in our Constitution, including the Charter of Rights and Freedoms. It will, however, dictate additional sharing of resources on the land, which will cause anxiety among present users. These changes must be approached from a base of love, not fear, and be founded on respect and a desire for a sustainable future for all future generations.

In 2019, Bill C-99 was introduced in Parliament in Ottawa. This is a new version of the citizenship oath that includes wording to respect Indigenous rights: "I swear (or affirm) that I will be faithful and bear true allegiance to Her Majesty Queen Elizabeth the Second, Queen of Canada, Her Heirs and Successors, and that I will faithfully observe the laws of Canada, including the Constitution, which recognizes and affirms the Aboriginal and treaty rights of First Nations, Inuit and Métis peoples, and fulfil my duties as a Canadian Citizen."

Senator Murray Sinclair, who chaired the Truth and Reconciliation Commission, commented on the proposed changes: "Reconciliation requires that a new vision, based on a commitment to mutual respect, be developed. Part of that vision is encouraging all Canadians, including newcomers, to understand the history of First Nations, the Métis and the Inuit, including information about the treaties and the history of the residential schools, so that we all honour the truth and work together to build a more inclusive Canada." Personally, I believe it is unfortunate that all Canadians, including those born in this country, do not swear an oath of citizenship or take the necessary test required of newcomers to become citizens of our nation.

There are some one and a half million Indigenous people self-identified in Canada, with over six hundred bands and many languages. They are as diverse as the rest of Canadians, and if you speak to individuals from First Nations communities across Canada, their opinions on the role of the Crown in Canada today will be as varied as those of other Canadians from coast to coast to coast. And just as the different nations have very diverse opinions on pipelines and fish farms, their answers will be coloured by their personal experiences and their physical locations.

The Queen's representatives in Ottawa and the provincial capitals have prerogative powers and the responsibility to ensure there is always a government and a first minister in office. Canadians are aware that this role, like many of the viceregal duties, is largely ceremonial and that the Crown's non-partisan, neutral position is seldom called upon; but just knowing these reserve powers exist is important and helps to maintain civility in our political institutions. It is a matter of respect. The connection, history, universality, civility, and honour represented by the Crown are a large part of our fabric. Like hereditary chiefs of many First Nations, the Crown is represented by sober, apolitical, elder statespersons, ready to advise elected politicians when necessary or to act as an adjudicator, and this represents a constraint.

The example of lifelong service and leadership demonstrated by our esteemed sovereign, over so many decades and through every trial that a nation or family could experience, is an incredible model that we are fortunate to have as guidance.

I am at the core a farmer and an environmentalist. I believe that today many share a common vision and whether we are Indigenous leaders, hereditary monarchs, or newcomers to Canada, we are fast realizing that we cannot continue to take from this land, this "small blue dot, our home," at such an extravagant rate and leave future generations to pay the price. In his most comprehensive work, *Harmony: A New Way of Looking at Our World*,[3] the Prince of Wales looks at the ancient, intimate relationship with nature. In the final chapter, on "Relationship," referring to the processes of nature, the prince says, "They are themselves the result of a rich biodiversity of life interacting with itself at many different levels. But for this finely tuned coherence to flourish, it needs to be nourished and respected, treated with reverence and considered sacred." In 1938, Charles Kellogg, a renowned American soil scientist, asked, "Do civilizations fail because soils fail to produce or does soil fail only when people living on it no longer know how to manage their civilization?"

We must use our collective talents and the greatest wisdom of all sectors of our society to solve the future challenges. We will need the traditional knowledge born of the long history and of place-based wisdom of the elders of the Indigenous Peoples. We will need the very best science of the research facilities and universities. We will need the leadership of our elected officials that allows us to collaborate and make policy based on sound science. We will also be inspired by examples set by monarchs. We will require adaptation and resilience, and we will need respect for the history both oral, as passed down through generations of Indigenous elders, and recorded by non-Indigenous Canadians, all those who have settled here and who make Canada home. We must strive to conserve our civil society, because only then will we be able to honour one another and to make the changes required of us. We want a future for all our children that is more than sustainable. As a wise man once said, "After all, would you want a sustainable marriage?" Richard Louv, author of *Last Child in the Woods*, when speaking at a birthday celebration for artist Robert Bateman, said, "We must create a vision of the future as seen through the eyes of Robert Bateman." We can do that when we learn to recognize and live with our past. Through that doorway we will build a healthy future for all Canadians.

We in Canada are so very fortunate because we live in this most blessed of nations where both our soils and our governance are young and vibrant. Our wise elders and our Queen symbolize a special quality, removed from the partisan nature of politics, and they demonstrate respect. Respect for the worthiness of *all* citizens and for all our planet's life-supporting systems. And so to all our children, the future leaders of our provinces and our nation, I will continue to preach that we must remain vigilant in guarding our precious soils *and* our constitutional monarchy so that this nation may remain vibrant and be passed to future generations as "the true north, strong and free."

Notes

1. Ronald Wright, *A Short History of Progress* (Toronto: House of Anansi Press, 2004).
2. Marcus Tullius Cicero, *How to Run a Country: An Ancient Guide for Modern Leaders*, trans. Philip Freeman (Princeton and Oxford: Princeton University Press, 2013).
3. HRH The Prince of Wales, with Tony Juniper and Ian Skelly, *Harmony: A New Way of Looking at Our World* (London: Harper Collins, 2010).

PART TWO

THE EVOLVING
VICEREGAL OFFICES

THE PROVINCIAL CROWN AND LIEUTENANT GOVERNORS

Andrew Heard

Both in theory and substance, Canada's sovereign is represented by eleven officials, with the governor general acting in the Queen's place for national government and a lieutenant governor representing the Queen in each of the provinces. And yet, such a description fails to capture the complexity and fluid history of the Crown in Canada.[1]

Canadian provincial governments have experienced a thorough metamorphosis in the years since Confederation in 1867. It may be hard for many Canadians in the twenty-first century to imagine this, but the provinces began life in the new Dominion of Canada as little more than glorified municipal governments in the eyes of both the Canadian and British governments. Along with key judicial decisions significantly restricting the original legislative powers of the national parliament while expanding the power of the provincial legislature, important shifts in political and cultural values led to a snowballing growth in Canadians' beliefs that the provinces mattered, both as societies and polities. Canada began life as a new dominion founded on a superior national government and subordinate provincial governments, but it has since transformed into a true federal system with two coordinate levels of government that are, at least in theory, autonomous in their assigned areas of jurisdiction. A key part of this "province-building" relied on fundamental changes in the role of the lieutenant governors and the acceptance of separate provincial Crowns.

This chapter explores the evolution of the provincial Crowns and the roles of the lieutenant governors who personify them. Embedded in this story is an almost Cinderella-like tale of lieutenant governors, who began life as federal servants but who eventually attended the royal ball. Yet it is a tale without the charmed ending at this point, as the lieutenant governors and provincial Crowns still remain subordinate in some ways to the governor general and the national Crown.

In political science terms, a federation is a system of government in which the national and regional governments are "coordinate," meaning none is subordinated to another. If all Canadian provinces were on an equal footing with the national government, then the Queen's eleven representatives would be of equal standing. Effectively, there would be eleven independent Crowns in Canada. In Australia this has long been the case. There, the state governors (equivalent to Canada's provincial lieutenant governors) are direct representatives of the Queen and the national government plays no role in either their appointment or their communications with the Queen.[2] In Canada, however, theory and practice have never provided such a clear picture. Indeed, for several decades after Confederation, the governor general was widely viewed as the Queen's *only* representative in Canada. Much has changed since then, and the story of the journey taken so far and the distance left to travel is well worth telling.

Canadian Federalism and Lieutenant Governors in the Early Years

While Canada has claimed to be a federation since 1867, this label is regarded by jurists and scholars as a misnomer when applied to the actual system of government originally created for Canada. Granted, the potential framework for a federation was provided for in the *Constitution Act, 1867* with powers assigned "exclusively" to the provincial legislatures and others assigned to the national government (originally called the dominion government). However, the overriding powers of the dominion government were not compatible with a true federation. The Judicial Committee of the Privy Council (Canada's highest court of appeal until 1949) once opined that the reference to Canada being "federally united" in the preamble to the Act was accurate only "in a loose sense," and not in the "natural and literal interpretation of the word."[3] And even as late as the mid-twentieth century, British scholar K.C. Wheare could only go so far as to describe Canada as a "quasi-federation" — and that was after decades of province-building through court cases and political actions to empower provincial governments.[4] But by the late twentieth and early twenty-first century, there could be no doubt that the Supreme Court of Canada was determined to enforce a vision of a classical federal system with two orders of government that are distinct and coordinate in status, despite the increasing degree of policy co-operation and intertwined administration they may practise.[5]

In the initial years of British rule in what became Canada, the provinces existed as colonies under the direct authority and legislative power of the monarch, as part of the royal prerogative. Once representative assemblies were established, they came under the legislative authority of the Westminster parliament while remaining under the executive authority of the British monarch. With Confederation, the three existing colonies were consolidated into one "dominion," which remained a colony, even if with more internal autonomy than other colonies in the empire. The original *British North America Act* of 1867 clearly continued the relationship with the British Crown. Not only did the preamble state that the Dominion of Canada would be "federally united under the Crown of the

United Kingdom of Great Britain and Ireland, with a Constitution similar in Principle to that of the United Kingdom," but section 5 also stipulated, "The Executive Government and Authority of and over Canada is hereby declared to continue and be vested in the Queen."

The story of the Crown in the provinces since 1867 is a story of both Canada's developing independence from Great Britain and of the provinces from the dominion government. While the preamble may have optimistically declared that the Dominion of Canada was to be "federally united," the nature of that federalism and the relationship between the provinces and the dominion government would prove in the early days to be not very federal at all. Indeed, the first decades of Confederation have been characterized as "colonial federalism."

The colonial relationship between the provinces and the national government mirrored in striking ways the relationship between the Canadian and British governments. Table 1 offers a quick visual summary of the parallels between the two subordinated relationships. The governor general and lieutenant governors were selected and appointed by a higher level of government without local input. And the governor general and lieutenant governors were required to act on formal instructions from the higher government. In functional terms, the governor general was there to represent imperial interests in Canada. The task of the governor general was to ensure that the Canadian dominion government understood British imperial priorities and Canadian policies did not conflict with British policies. By the same token, the task of the lieutenant governors was to represent the dominion government's interests in the provinces by ensuring the provincial policies did not conflict with national policies.

The governor general had to report to the British government on Canadian political affairs and would convey to the Canadian government any British concerns. Similarly, the lieutenant governors reported to the Canadian government on affairs in their provinces and had to present national government concerns to their provincial ministers. The ministers in the superior level of government to whom the governor general and lieutenant governors had to report even had a similar ring to their titles. The governor general reported to the Secretary of State for the Colonies, while the lieutenant governors reported to the Secretary of State for the Provinces.

Both the national parliament and provincial legislatures were subordinated to a higher level of authority. Powers of reservation and disallowance ensured that the British government could scrutinize and veto any legislation passed by the Canadian parliament, and the Canadian government could veto any provincial legislation it did not approve of. In practice, the subjugation of the provinces to dominion government authority was even more pronounced in the matter of reservation and disallowance of legislation than the dominion government was to the British government. Over the years a total of 168 provincial bills were disallowed or refused assent by the governor general acting on the advice of the national cabinet.[6] In contrast, the British government vetoed only seven bills from the Canadian parliament.[7]

In the first few decades after Confederation, the only accepted representative of the Crown in Canada was the governor general. The lieutenant governors were viewed as agents of the federal government, not

Table 1. **A Tale of Two Colonial Relationships**

Dominion of Canada

- GG appointed by the Queen, subject to U.K. government instructions
- GG reported to U.K. government on dominion policies
- GG ensured dominion policies did not conflict with imperial policies
- Reservation & disallowance of legislation passed by Canadian parliament

Provinces of Canada

- LGs appointed by GG, subject to dominion government instructions
- LG reported to dominion government on provincial policies
- LG ensured provincial policies did not conflict with dominion policies
- Reservation & disallowance of legislation passed by provincial legislatures

representatives of the Crown. As John Saywell described the situation, "The Lieutenant Governor is a federal officer, appointed, paid, dismissable, and instructed, by the federal government. His position as a federal officer was in principle identical to that of the colonial governor as an imperial officer."[8] The status of the lieutenant governors and the question of whether the Queen was in any way involved in provincial government were both hotly contested in a series of court cases over the late nineteenth and early twentieth centuries.[9]

The constitutional framework for the governor general and lieutenant governors contains some clear distinctions in wording that are worth noting. In particular, the governor general was for many decades after Confederation appointed by the Queen under letters patent and commissions sealed with the sign manual, a personal seal of the monarch.[10] In contrast, lieutenant governors are formally appointed by the governor general in council, not by the governor general acting personally.[11] The council advising the governor general is named as "the Queen's Privy Council for Canada" according to section 11 of the *Constitution Act, 1867*, while the provincial equivalents are simply known as the executive council. As well, the Act makes a distinction between the locus of legislative power for the national and provincial legislatures. Section 17 states, "There shall be One Parliament for Canada, consisting of the Queen, an Upper House styled the Senate, and the House of Commons." And in section 91 the powers of Parliament are introduced with the phrase, "It shall be lawful for the Queen, by and with the Advice and Consent of the Senate and House of Commons, to make laws ..." Quite clearly, the Queen was intended to be an integral part of Canada's national parliament, and the legislative power is symbolically vested in the Queen acting on the advice of the two houses of Parliament. In granting royal assent to bills approved by the Senate and House of Commons, the governor general is clearly acting in the place of the Queen. The references in the Act to the provincial legislatures are of a quite different character and make no mention of the Queen. The new provincial legislatures created for Ontario and Quebec were declared to consist of the lieutenant governor and houses of the assembly.[12]

Initially, the courts ruled in favour of the position taken by the Canadian and British governments, that the Queen was absent from provincial government and that lieutenant governors were, in essence, representatives of the Canadian government and not the Queen. An 1875 decision of the Ontario Court of Queen's Bench held that lieutenant governors did not possess the prerogative powers of the Crown, and therefore could not authorize special courts. Chief Justice Harrison wrote that this "power being a prerogative one can only be exercised by the Queen or her representative. The Governor General is the only officer … who answers this description."[13] In *Lenoir v. Ritchie* (1879), the Supreme Court of Canada struck down Nova Scotian legislation assigning precedence for lawyers named as Queen's Counsel by the lieutenant governor.[14] The court ruled that the granting of honours was a prerogative of the Crown, and the Queen was neither a part of the Nova Scotia legislature nor represented in Nova Scotia by the lieutenant governor. As Justice Taschereau described the lieutenant governors, "They are officers of the dominion government. Their office, as heads of the provinces, is a very high and a very honourable one indeed, but they are not Her Majesty's representatives, at least quo ad the matter now under consideration …"[15] And Justice Gwynne said in the same case:

> The Dominion of Canada is constituted a quasi-imperial power, in which Her Majesty retains all her executive and legislative authority in all matters not placed under the executive control of the provincial authorities, in the same manner as she does in the British Isles; while the Provincial Governments are, as it were, carved out of and subordinated to the Dominion Government. The head of their executive Government is not an officer appointed by Her Majesty, or holding any commission from her, or in any manner personally representing her, but an officer of the Dominion Government.… The Queen forms no part of the Provincial Legislatures, as she does of the Dominion Parliament.[16]

A further diminution of the provinces and lieutenant governors came from the Supreme Court in the 1881 *Mercer* case, in which the court held that the right of the Crown to receive estates of individuals who die intestate was a prerogative right that could not belong to the lieutenant governors.[17] Justices Taschereau and Gwynne revisited and reinforced the views they had expressed in *Lenoir v. Ritchie* that the provinces were subordinate levels of government and the lieutenant governors were not general representatives of the Queen.

This consistent subordination of lieutenant governors and provincial governments did not sit well with most provincial premiers.[18] At a gathering of five premiers at the Inter-Provincial Conference of 1887, a resolution was passed on the role of lieutenant governors:

> That it was the intention of the British North America Act, and of the Provinces which were thereby confederated, that in respect of all matters as to which the Provincial Legislatures have authority the Lieutenant Governor of every Province, as the Representative of the Sovereign in Provincial affairs, should have the same Executive authority as other Governors and Lieutenant-Governors of British Colonies and Provinces.

In other words, the Canadian lieutenant governors should be able to exercise all prerogative powers of the Crown relevant to provincial governance.[19]

The Crown Established as Part of Provincial Government

The debate in Canada over the status and powers of lieutenant governors and of provincial governments was shifted into a fresh dimension with a watershed ruling in London by the Judicial Committee of the Privy Council in 1892. The British judges who decided the *Liquidators of the Maritime Bank* case came down squarely on the side of the provinces.[20] This case was about the order of precedence of creditors in a bankruptcy, with the Canadian government arguing that it was the sole representative of the Crown in Canada and therefore provincial governments could claim no prerogative right to a division of assets ahead of other creditors in a bankruptcy. In dismissing this argument, Lord Watson first dispensed with the notion that provinces were subordinate bodies: "The object of the Act was neither to weld the provinces into one, nor to subordinate provincial governments to a central authority, but to create a federal government in which they should all be represented, entrusted with the exclusive administration of affairs in which they had a common interest, each province retaining its independence and autonomy."[21]

The most crucial part of the ruling was a definitive statement on the status of the lieutenant governors as representatives of the Crown: "The act of the Governor-General and his Council in making the appointments is, within the meaning of the statute, the act of the Crown; and a Lieutenant-Governor, when appointed, is as much the representative of Her Majesty for all purposes of provincial government as the Governor-General himself is for all purposes of Dominion government."[22]

This clear statement on the role of lieutenant governors as representatives of the Crown was followed by further court cases cementing the Crown into provincial government. In 1916, the Judicial Committee of the Privy Council ruled in *Bonanza Creek Gold Mining Co. v. The King* that the prerogative powers of the Crown were divided to match the legislative powers of the federal and provincial governments.[23] Therefore, the provinces had all the prerogative powers necessary to their areas of legislative jurisdiction.

Two other cases explicitly rejected older views that the Queen was not a part of provincial legislatures. In 1919, the Judicial Committee echoed its position on the status of provincial governments from the *Maritime Bank* case:

> The scheme of the Act passed in 1867 was thus, not to weld the Provinces into one, nor to subordinate Provincial Governments to a central authority, but to establish a central government in which these Provinces should be represented, entrusted with exclusive authority only in affairs in which they had a common interest. Subject to this each Province was to retain its independence and autonomy and to be directly under the Crown as its head.[24]

The opinion then went on to add, "The Lieutenant Governor who represents the Sovereign is part of the Legislature."[25] The Supreme Court of Canada then further reiterated in 1938 that the Crown was a tangible part of the provincial legislative process through the participation of the lieutenant governor: "The act of a Lieutenant-Governor in assenting to a bill or in reserving a bill is the act of the Crown by the Crown's representative just as the act of the Governor General in assenting to a bill or reserving a bill is the act of the Crown."[26]

The inherent role of the sovereign in the provincial legislative process is symbolized in the legislative enactment phrase used in six provinces at the beginning of all their acts. This is illustrated by Manitoba's act: "Her Majesty, by and with the advice and consent of the Legislative Assembly of Manitoba, enacts as follows …"[27] Interestingly, three of the Atlantic provinces use legislative enactment phrases originating prior to Confederation; in Nova Scotia's case the phrase used in provincial statutes is "Be it enacted by the Governor and Assembly as follows …"[28] Quebec now uses the most generic enacting phrase: "The Parliament of Québec enacts as follows …"

Regardless of whether the Queen is mentioned or not in the enacting phrases of legislation, the law seems settled at this point that in assenting to legislation the lieutenant governor is technically granting royal assent on behalf of the sovereign.[29] In this respect there has been a fundamental shift from the early years of Confederation, when not just Canadian and British ministers but the Supreme Court of Canada as well believed that the Queen had no role in provincial legislatures, any more than she did in municipal government.

In a case in 1948, *The King v. Caroll*, the Supreme Court of Canada also put paid to the notion that, in law, lieutenant governors are officials of the federal government simply because they are appointed, paid, and may be instructed by the federal government; once appointed, the court ruled, lieutenant governors are officials of their provincial governments.[30] The case involved a retired judge who was appointed to be lieutenant governor and denied his judicial pension on the grounds that the *Judges Act* prohibited paying the pension while a retiree holds a public office under the Government of Canada. Writing for the majority, Justice Robert Taschereau said:

The nature of the federal and provincial legislative and executive powers is clearly settled, and a Lieutenant-Governor, who "carries on the Government of the Province", manifestly does not act in respect of the Government of Canada. All the functions he performs are directed to the affairs of the Province and are in no way connected with the Government of Canada, and it is the functions that he performs that must be examined in order to determine the nature of his office.[31]

Thus provincial governments have been substantially elevated in power and status since the early years of Confederation, with the courts playing a crucial role in establishing that, as a matter of law, the Crown is present in provincial government. Political developments, however, were slow following the Judicial Committee's groundbreaking ruling in *Liquidators of the Maritime Bank*, with the federal government continuing for decades to instruct lieutenant governors on the reservation and disallowance of provincial legislation not approved by Ottawa. But ripples from the case continued to build over the years, until it became irrefutable that the lieutenant governors are not only symbolic representatives of the Queen in provincial government but also must possess the corresponding royal prerogatives necessary to provincial governance. These developments also reflected the notion of separate legal personas for the Crown within Canada's federation, as it is necessary for each government to be able to represent itself independently in court, especially when two (or more) are litigating against each other. The legal phrase often used is the "Queen in right of" a jurisdiction, for example, "the Queen in right of Alberta," and "the Queen in right of Canada."

The notion of a divisible Crown was essential not only to the evolution of Canada's federal system but to the transformation of the British Empire, just as there was once thought to be a single Crown across the entire British Empire and it became necessary to accept that the Queen in right of Australia was a separate legal entity from the Queen in right of New Zealand or of the United Kingdom.[32] But there is a significant difference between how the divided Crown occurred within Canada and the division of the Crown across the empire. While from the beginning it was accepted that the sovereign formed a part of the colonial governing structures across the empire, in the early decades of Canada's federation the Queen was said not to be a part of provincial government — being an integral part of only the national government in Canada. For the Crown to become divided federally in Canada, it was first necessary for the courts to inject the Crown into provincial governments.

Individual but Not Coordinate Crowns

Despite the judicial infusion of the Crown into provincial government in Canada, little has changed in the hierarchy of Canadian governments and their relations with the sovereign. Canada has never had a condition where all federal and provincial Crowns are coordinate, as illustrated in Figure 1. Figure 2 depicts how the layers of government and channels of communication were actually arranged from 1867 until 1930. During that time, British ministers alone were able to directly communicate with and advise the sovereign on matters across the entire empire. As mentioned above, Canada initially remained just another part of the empire, under the authority of the British government and Crown, despite its creation as a "dominion" in 1867 with substantial autonomy in domestic affairs. Provincial governments and lieutenant governors could communicate with higher authorities only through the federal government; if issues needed to be raised with the British government or the sovereign, then those matters had to pass through the federal cabinet and the governor general would relay the matter to British ministers. Even after the judicial decisions establishing that the lieutenant governors were in fact representatives of the monarch, nothing changed in the necessity to follow these hierarchical stages of communications.

The first significant change in the channels of communication occurred after the 1930 Imperial Conference, held between the British government and ministers from Canada and the other dominions. At the 1930 conference, it was agreed that dominion ministers would henceforth be the ministers who would advise the King on the appointment of new governors

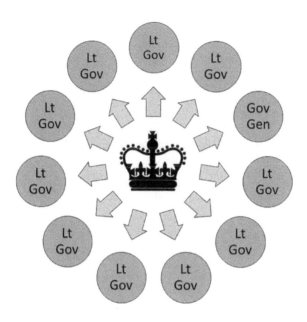

FIGURE 1. Diagram of ideal relations among Canada's Crowns, if they were all equal and coordinate.

general and all other dominion affairs. But the British government did not entirely relinquish its role in advising the King on matters impacting the entire empire, or "Commonwealth," as it came to be known. In Canada's case, the role for British ministers to advise the monarch remained until the passage of the *Canada Act, 1982*, when Canada finally established its own domestic procedures to amend its Constitution. Until that point, many changes to Canada's formal constitutional documents involved asking the British government to pass the necessary legislation. As a result, the British government had an integral role to play in informing and advising the Queen on such requests and consequent parliamentary developments; Figure 3 illustrates the relationship and channels of communication from 1930 onwards.

In recent years, there has been one substantial development in the lieutenant governors' ability to communicate directly with the royals. Although lieutenant governors to this day must channel virtually all contacts with the

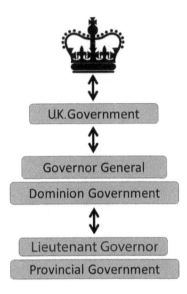

FIGURE 2. Diagram of the hierarchy of relationships and channels of communication, 1867 to 1930.

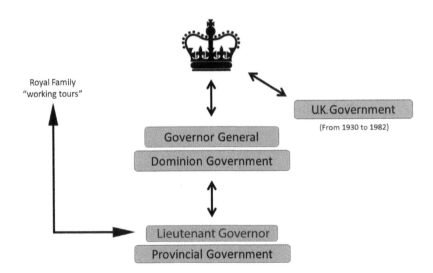

FIGURE 3. Diagram of the hierarchy of relationships and channels of communication, 1930 to the present.

Queen and the Prince of Wales through the governor general's office, some lieutenant governors have started to communicate directly with the households of other members of the royal family to organize "working visits" in their provinces.[33] Official royal tours by the Queen, the Prince of Wales, and the Duke of Cambridge (Prince William) are now outnumbered by trips involving other members of the royal family such as the Princess Royal (Princess Anne), the Duke of York (Prince Andrew), and the Earl of Wessex (Prince Edward). Although the rationale for these working visits involves meetings with the charities or military units with which a royal may have connections, they may also allow for public appearances and meetings with provincial dignitaries and the general public. Depending on the degree and nature of the public appearances, the premier's office and protocol office are involved in the planning, and in a number of provinces, for example, Saskatchewan,[34] take the lead as a matter of course. Where the lieutenant governor's office takes the lead in a working visit, it helps raise their status and cement a direct connection to the sovereign and royal family. For example, during his 2019 visit to Nova Scotia, the Duke of York was hosted by the lieutenant governor while staying at Government House. Given the number of working visits and the engagement with Canadians that comes with them, these visits provide valuable opportunities to raise the profile of the Crown in the provinces.

An ongoing question mark hangs over the current degree to which lieutenant governors remain subordinated to the status and authority of the governor general. In a recent annual meeting with the lieutenant governors, a governor general made a point of stressing that they were all representatives of the Queen, parts of a "family" engaged in a common mission to promote the Crown. But while such a statement may strike some as a description of equals, it is interesting to see how that sentiment actually plays out in practice. Certainly, past behaviour by previous governors general has firmly imprinted a hierarchy among those representing the sovereign in Canada. It is not many years since a governor general was preceded into this annual meeting of viceregal representatives by the secretary, who announced ostentatiously, "Please rise for the Governor General of Canada." Quite correctly, several lieutenant governors did not rise, as all were equally representatives of the Queen. While the changing occupants of Rideau Hall have varied in asserting a privileged position relative to the lieutenant governors, the trend in the modern era is of governors general viewing themselves at least as "first among equals," and, if there is a Canadian family of viceregals, usually as the parental unit. On the other hand, some have explicitly asserted that they are the head of state of Canada, firmly demoting lieutenant governors well beneath them.

Regardless of collegial rhetoric from individual governors general, there are myriad ways in which lieutenant governors are subordinated to the governor general and the federal government. Most symbolic is the insistence that only the governor general's office may initiate communication with the Queen and the next in line to the throne.[35] Even when a matter solely concerns issues between a province and the sovereign, a request must be made to initiate the contact; with that comes the opportunity for a refusal. The deliberate reservation for the governor general of the royal prerogative powers relating to foreign relations is another unambiguous assertion of the primacy of the governor general, putting the Queen's mantle of head of state on the shoulders of the governor general to wear on a daily basis. Another illustration of the symbolic subordination of lieutenant governors is the insistence that governors general receive the same number of gun salutes as the Queen (twenty-one) while lieutenant governors receive significantly less (fifteen); it is interesting to note that the Queen's provincial representatives are entitled to fewer guns than either the prime minister (nineteen) or the minister of defence (seventeen).[36] The exclusive use of "Your Excellency" for addressing a governor general contrasts with the use of "Your Honour" for lieutenant governors.[37] The federal order of protocol clearly declares the superior position of the governor general: "The Governor General, under all circumstances, should be accorded precedence immediately after the Sovereign."[38] The table of precedence normally places lieutenant governors well down the list of public officials.

At Canadian government events, lieutenant governors occupy the ninth rung in the order of precedence, below the governor general and spouse, the prime minister, chief justice of Canada, the speakers of the Senate and House of Commons, ambassadors, members of the federal cabinet, and the leader of the opposition. If the governor general is not attending, a lieutenant governor would rise in precedence to be next after the prime minister — still subordinated to a federal politician despite being the only direct representative of the sovereign present. Provincial governments have their own tables of precedence, which vary considerably. Saskatchewan is the only province to explicitly refer to the governor general and prime minister, who take precedence right after the lieutenant governor and premier when attending a provincial function.[39] Manitoba, perhaps unintentionally, offers a symbolic acquiescence to the federal Crown by according members of the Privy Council of Canada resident in Manitoba a higher precedence than members of the province's own executive council.[40] Several other provinces rank members of the Privy Council lower than those of their executive council.[41] Quebec makes no mention at all of federal officials in its order of precedence.[42]

The lieutenant governors are also beholden to the federal government in several practical ways. First and foremost, the federal government continues to select and appoint lieutenant governors with little to no input from the provinces. Second, the federal government pays the lieutenant governors' salaries. Third, the lieutenant governors are still issued instructions by the federal government.[43] While mostly benign, they include a command subordinating their freedom of movement to a federal minister's discretion: "The Lieutenant Governor shall not quit the Province without having first informed the Minister of Canadian Heritage of her intended absence, and must not leave Canada in her official capacity without having first obtained leave for so doing through the Minister of Canadian Heritage."[44] The federal government, through the department of Canadian Heritage, also subsidizes certain expenses for the lieutenant governors' office (including the trip to meet the Queen once during their term of office). It should be noted, however, that federal funds are also a safeguard of lieutenant governors and the provincial Crown against cost-cutting or anti-monarchist provincial governments.[45]

Official royal tours of the Queen or of the Prince of Wales are negotiated and cost-shared between federal and provincial committees, usually involving the lieutenant governor's office, the protocol office, and the premier's office at the provincial level, and ultimately approved by the minister of Canadian Heritage, with the involvement of the secretary to the governor general. At times, the primacy of the federal Crown is quite evident in the planning of royal tours, as aspects of provincial plans for a royal tour have been vetoed by federal officials. British Columbia was refused a request for the Queen to open the provincial legislature in 1964, and in 2005 Alberta was unable to get agreement for the Queen to grant royal assent to a bill during her 2005 visit. One reason given by the secretary to the governor general for the 2005 refusal was that such an action by the Queen "would not be consistent with the long-standing Canadianization of our institutions."[46] In a throwback to the earlier argument over whether the Queen is a part of the provincial legislatures, it has been argued that it would be better to refuse the request on the grounds that the Queen is only symbolically, not personally, part of the legislature and cannot therefore personally give royal assent, even if the lieutenant governor does so in her name.[47] However, it does seem odd to argue that the sovereign cannot perform the actions done in her name by others as her representative when the Judicial Committee of the Privy Council wrote in 1919, "For when the Lieutenant-Governor gives to or withholds his assent from a Bill passed by the Legislature of the Province, it is in contemplation of law the Sovereign that so gives or withholds assent."[48] The disparity in the federal authorities' regard for the sovereign's connection with the provincial legislatures compared to the national parliament is seen in the fact that King George VI granted assent to nine bills in Ottawa during the 1939 royal visit and the Queen delivered the speech from the throne there in 1957 and again in 1977.

The primacy of the governor general is sometimes defended on the basis that the 1947 Letters Patent issued by King George VI authorized the governor general "to exercise all powers and authorities lawfully belonging to Us in respect of Canada."[49] For some, this means the governor general may act in the Queen's place with respect to any and all issues within Canada, perhaps including provincial matters when needed. However, there are several considerations that would appear to prohibit the monarch from delegating any powers of the provincial Crowns to the governor general. The first is that the *Constitution Act, 1867* gives clarity in the division of roles between the governor general, stated in section 10 to be "an officer carrying on the Government of Canada," and a lieutenant governor, whom section 62 refers to as "an officer carrying on the Government of the Province."[50]

Lieutenant governors and the governor general are chief executive officers of two completely different sets of governments. A second consideration is that the letters patent were drafted by the federal cabinet under Prime Minister Louis St. Laurent without provincial consultation. A third issue is that the full text of article 2 delegating the Queen's powers to the governor general states that these powers are to be exercised by the governor general "with the advice of Our Privy Council for Canada or of any members thereof or individually, as the case requires."[51]

Most importantly, however, the monarch cannot use a prerogative instrument, such as letters patent, to alter the federal system. The courts have interpreted the *Constitution Act, 1867* and related documents to create a federal system of government with distinct executive powers for each of the federal and provincial governments. Given the courts' clear ruling that the executive powers relating to provincial government are attached to the provincial Crown, there is little chance that the Supreme Court of Canada would agree that the sovereign could, on the federal cabinet's advice, issue a prerogative document to delegate any of the Queen's provincial powers to the federal government. To admit this were possible would do serious damage to the federalism principle. The sovereign's powers "in respect of Canada" that have been delegated to the governor general can only be those powers relating to the federal level of government and not the entire Dominion of Canada.[52]

Despite this pattern of subordination, there is much potential to build on the status and prestige of the provincial Crown and lieutenant governor. Either as an act of province-building or simply to promote a province's direct connection with the monarchy, provincial governments could follow the example of federal government campaigns in the first half of the twentieth century to wrest control of their royal institutions from the British. Just as the Canadian government did, provincial governments could campaign to take the lead in nominating suitable candidates to the prime minister for their viceregal officers. Just as Quebec informally gained a lead role in 2019 under the Trudeau government in nominating Supreme Court of Canada justices from that province, so too could those provincial governments who desire to be given the initiative in selections for lieutenant governor; however, such a move would best involve an independent provincial nominating committee, to preclude patronage considerations. Provincial governments could encourage the lieutenant governors to communicate directly with the Queen, just as governors general stopped communicating with the monarch through British officials. Provincial governments could follow the example of Australian state practice and address their lieutenant governors as "Your Excellency"; as direct representatives of the Queen they should be entitled to that style of address.[53] Similarly, lieutenant governors should be entitled to the same number of gun salutes as the governor general. Provincial premiers could start referring to their viceregal officers as "Governor" instead of the inherently diminutive "Lieutenant Governor," although the formal title could not be changed without a constitutional amendment.[54]

A provincial government could go further and accord the Queen an official title for the province. Saskatchewan took one step down this path when its lieutenant governor issued a proclamation on the Queen's accession to the throne, referring to her as "Supreme Liege Lady in and Over Saskatchewan."[55] While the Canadian parliament passed the *Royal Style and Titles Act*[56] in 1953 to create the title of Queen of Canada, this measure is in effect only an official "Hello My Name Is" sticker. And it should not preclude a province from passing its own equivalent measure to give an official provincial title, such as, say, Queen of British Columbia, just as the Queen has official titles for Australian states.[57] In law there are already separate Crowns in right of each province and it is not unconstitutional to propose separate titles for Her Majesty to go with that reality. A title is just an official name plaque, not an alteration to the office of the Queen, let alone the creation of a provincial office of the Queen.[58] Over the course of the twentieth century Canadian governments successfully created a localized cultural and political identity for the Queen as Queen of Canada.[59] It should be open to provincial governments to do the same.

Choosing Lieutenant Governors

Key to building the profile and identity of the provincial Crown are the quality and conduct of individuals appointed to be lieutenant governors. For many decades following Confederation, the federal government tended to appoint sympathetic partisans, often former MLAs and MPs, who could further the federal government's agenda with the provincial governments, through persuasion and, if necessary, reservation of provincial legislation. Between 1867 and 1988, at least 138 of the 211 lieutenant governors had previously held elected office; this number does not include financial backers and party organizers.[60] In the late twentieth century an appreciation developed for nonpartisan appointees, or at least those with partisan backgrounds who could act with neutral statesmanship. Lieutenant governor of Ontario Lincoln Alexander is a prime example of someone who was widely respected for his neutrality in office despite his partisan history, and Saskatchewan's NDP premier Roy Romanow valued his private meetings with Lieutenant Governor Jack Wiebe, despite the latter having been a Liberal MLA. However Alberta's Conservative premier Peter Lougheed reportedly became more guarded with his lieutenant governor after a former Liberal candidate was appointed.[61] Not all appointees have been successes, with some guilty of wrongdoing in office while others pursued business or political connections while in office. The most unfortunate example of viceregal wrongdoing is seen in the 2015 criminal conviction of Lise Thibault for breach of trust and fraud for over $640,000 of inappropriate spending and expense claims while Quebec's lieutenant governor.[62]

In 2010, Prime Minister Stephen Harper appointed an expert committee to advise him on the choice of a successor to Governor General Michaëlle Jean. The result was the highly praised choice of David Johnston, who continued in office until 2017. In an effort to ensure similar competent and nonpartisan appointments of provincial lieutenant governors and territorial commissioners, Harper established an independent advisory committee on viceregal appointments in 2012 to identify suitable candidates. Despite this process being widely regarded as a success, Prime Minister Justin Trudeau scrapped the advisory committee after his election in 2015 and handed the selection process back to the Prime Minister's Office. The result has been the return of partisan patronage, with three of the six individuals appointed by mid-2019 having recently donated to either the federal or provincial Liberal parties; one was even a recent member of Prime Minister Trudeau's cabinet.

Unfortunately, allegations of continued partisan connections later surfaced in connection with at least one of these appointees. Such incidents risk undermining the integrity of the position and do little to further the public's confidence in the lieutenant governor's neutrality if that person is called on to settle issues following an election where no one party wins a majority. In devising a process for appointing viceregal officials, it is important for politicians to remember that this concerns the selection of personal representatives of the Queen, who has spent a lifetime cultivating complete partisan neutrality. She is aware that her credibility and legitimacy when exercising the reserve powers in times of political and constitutional crisis depend on public confidence that she is a neutral actor. It seems incongruous, to say the least, that governments believe it is acceptable to choose partisan supporters to represent the steadfastly nonpartisan sovereign.

The importance of lieutenant governors who are seen to be nonpartisan is essential to the two broad roles of the office, constitutional and symbolic. The office was continued after Confederation only because a parliamentary system of government requires a separate head of state from head of government. The Queen, governor general, and lieutenant governors all owe their existence to this necessity; while the Queen is the head of state over all Canada, the governor general and lieutenant governors act as chief executive officers in her place for the purposes of federal and provincial government.[63] It should be noted that even republican parliamentary systems have separate offices of head of state and head of government. The inherent fragility of premiers owing their right to govern to first winning and then to maintaining the confidence of the elected members of the legislature means that some official may be needed to sort out who has the right to form a government after an election where no one party wins a majority; a loss of confidence early after an election may also raise the question of who else might be able to win the legislature's confidence and form a government. But the constitutional role of the lieutenant governors extends beyond this power.[64]

The reserve powers of the Crown entail a broader right, in rare circumstances, to dismiss a premier for gross misbehaviour, unconstitutional actions, or for clinging to office despite a clear loss of confidence. As well, Canadian governors are recognized as having a broader role to play as guardians of the Constitution, who may at times refuse to act on unconstitutional advice from their first ministers and cabinets. The reserve powers also include the possibility of insisting on the dissolution or summoning of the legislature; a dysfunctional legislature may have to be dissolved for a general election to resolve some deep political paralysis, and a legislature may have to be recalled if a government tries to govern for too long without the legislature in session.

The constitutional importance of ensuring continuity in office of the chief executives of provincial governments was finally recognized in 2017, when the federal cabinet authorized generic orders in council for the first time to provide for a set list of officials, one of whom may be chosen as an administrator to replace a lieutenant governor who is unable to perform the duties of the office through "absence, illness, or other inability."[65] Previously, an administrator was appointed only on an ad hoc, limited-term basis, by the federal government, as the need arose, which could leave a lacuna in provincial government during a time-sensitive crisis. This apparent inability to provide for an administrator to act on the death of a lieutenant governor puts the provincial Crowns at a disadvantage compared to the national Crown.[66] The 1947 Letters Patent explicitly provide for the chief justice, or other senior judge, to act as administrator in the event of the governor general's death.[67] The sudden death of a lieutenant governor poses a serious problem, as the federal government has to recruit and appoint a suitable new lieutenant governor, which can take time. In the meantime, there is no one to sign orders in council or grant royal assent to urgent legislation. For example, when Alberta's lieutenant governor Lois Hole died in office in 2005, the province was left without anyone to sign official papers for a two-week period; provincial government was in danger of literally grinding to a halt.[68] The same scenario played out again in July 2019, with thirteen days passing between the death of Saskatchewan's lieutenant governor, Thomas Molloy, and the appointment of his successor, Russell Mirasty. Even when the imminent demise was expected, the federal government delayed appointing a successor until after the funeral of the deceased governor; while designed as a show of respect, this policy placed politeness above the very real need for continuity in office of the highest position in provincial government. A similar issue arose the following month with the death of Jocelyn Roy Vienneau, lieutenant governor of New Brunswick. The appointment of Roy Vienneau's successor, Brenda Murphy, was announced on September 5, leaving the province without a lieutenant governor for more than a month.

In exercising these reserve powers in their constitutional role, lieutenant governors can only act effectively if the political actors involved, as well as the general public, have confidence in their political neutrality. The Achilles heel of anyone who accepts a viceregal position despite a clear association with one of the political parties is that they risk the easy criticism that they are either rewarding their own party or punishing its opponents. Judith Guichon was able to stickhandle the contentious issues following the 2017 election in British Columbia precisely because she was viewed as nonpartisan. Guichon was faced with an incumbent premier, Christy Clark, a Liberal, who tried to secure fresh elections after being defeated on a confidence motion immediately following the election. The problem was that the NDPs and Greens between them had won a bare majority of seats and had signed an agreement for the Greens to support an NDP minority government. With an alternative government in the wings, it would have been completely improper to authorize fresh elections rather than allow the formation of a new government.[69]

In addition, the lieutenant governors may claim the rights Walter Bagehot first ascribed to the Queen, "the right to be consulted, the right to encourage, and the right to warn."[70] Crucial to these rights is the ability of lieutenant governors to meet and discuss matters privately with their premiers. While some lieutenant governors are given a regular opportunity to do so, others are simply ignored by their premiers outside of public functions; Manitoban premiers reportedly have not met privately with their lieutenant governors since the 1960s.[71]

Lieutenant governors also fulfill very important symbolic roles that in fact consume far more of their time than any occasional constitutional duties.[72] As representatives of the Crown in their provinces, viceregal officers are supposed to personify the provincial society and polity as someone who is above politics and who can appeal to all in their community. The separation of their office from the premier's has the beneficial effect, as well, of placing a nonpartisan position above the politicians of the day, as a reminder that the premier, cabinet ministers, and members of the legislature all serve their province. Lieutenant governors have considerable opportunities to engage with the people of their province in visiting and publicly acknowledging various cultural and charitable groups. The provincial honours systems founded on the royal prerogative of the lieutenant governor provide another opportunity for the viceregal officers to engage and celebrate their province impartially, although in a number of provinces the honours system has taken on partisan overtones by involving the premier or executive council in the process.[73] A number of lieutenant governors have used their time in office to highlight particular needs in a society, such as literacy or mental health, and to organize fundraising and charitable relief for those in need. For example, James Bartleman in Ontario focused on reading initiatives in remote First Nations communities, creating an initiative that has continued to expand in the years since his time in office.[74] A lieutenant governor of British Columbia, Steven Point, launched a similar literacy project, "Write to Read," which also continues to this day. British Columbia's Government House Foundation, founded in 1987 with an initial focus on fundraising to preserve the historic residence of the lieutenant governor, has evolved to support a range of projects in the general community.[75] In all these symbolic activities the lieutenant governor's success depends on being embraced as someone above politics, which is another reason individuals with recent partisan connections are best not selected and would do well to decline if approached to become lieutenant governor.

Conclusion

Canada has witnessed a remarkable transformation of provincial governments and their lieutenant governors since Confederation. While at first regarded as little more than municipal governments, subordinated to the national government and headed by lieutenant governors acting as federal agents, provincial governments have evolved into autonomous polities and the lieutenant governors acknowledged as personal representatives of the Queen. In the beginning, the Crown was thought to be integral only to the national government and the governor general was the sole representative of the monarch in Canada. A series of judicial decisions essentially injected the Crown into provincial government, weaving the Queen into provincial legislatures and establishing that the lieutenant governors are not representatives of the federal government but of the Queen. The royal prerogatives of the Crown were determined to be fully exercisable by the governor general and lieutenant governors alike. And yet this judicial levelling has not resulted in equality among viceregal officials. Lieutenant governors remain subordinated in a number of ways, both symbolically and in practice. This degree of hierarchy is not required in a federal monarchy, as evidenced by the very different experience in Australia.

There is, however, much that could be done to elevate the status of lieutenant governors. If provincial governments had the will to build their provincial identity and foster their autonomy within the federation, they could emulate many of the steps taken by federal governments in the twentieth century to localize the monarchy, creating a new conception of our Queen as the Queen of Canada. There is creative room to further root the monarchy in each province and give proper status to the lieutenant governors who represent the Queen. And as personal representatives of the Crown, whose basic task is to inspire and engage all in their province, lieutenant governors should be chosen with suitable backgrounds to appear, like the Queen, to be above the political fray.

Notes

1. The author is indebted to the kind assistance of D. Michael Jackson and Christopher McCreery in researching and refining this chapter.

2. See Anne Twomey, *The Chameleon Crown: The Queen and Her Australian Governors* (New South Wales: Federation Press, 2006); and Peter Boyce, "Six State Monarchies," chap. 7 in *The Queen's Other Realms: The Crown and Its Legacy in Australia, Canada and New Zealand* (New South Wales: Federation Press, 2008).

3. *Attorney General for Commonwealth of Australia and others v. The Colonial Sugar Refining Company, Limited, and others*, [1913] UPCC 76 at 10; bailii.org/uk/cases/UKPC/1913/1913_76.pdf.

4. K.C. Wheare, *Federal Government*, 4th ed. (Oxford: Oxford University Press, 1963), 18–19.

5. The court's enforcement of the federal principle can be traced over a series of cases, including: *Reference re Resolution to Amend the Constitution*, [1981] 1 S.C.R. 753; *Reference re Secession of Quebec*, [1998] 2 S.C.R. 217; *Reference re Supreme Court Act*, 2014 SCC 21, s. 5–6; and *Reference re Senate Reform* 2014 SCC 32.

6. Lieutenant governors reserved a total of seventy bills, some on instruction and some on their own initiative, and the national cabinet advised the governor general to refuse to grant royal assent in fourteen of these cases; in addition, the governor general acted on cabinet advice to disallow 112 provincial acts that had been assented to by lieutenant governors. Only after the Second World War did the powers of reservation and disallowance become essentially nullified through constitutional conventions protecting the autonomy of the provinces. See Andrew Heard, *Canadian Constitutional Conventions: The Marriage of Law and Politics*, 2nd ed. (Toronto: Oxford University Press Canada, 2014), 157.

7. Governors general reserved twenty-one bills, and the British government advised the Queen to refuse assent in six of these instances (all occurring prior to 1878); the British government advised the Queen to disallow only one act assented to by the governor general, in 1873. See Peter W. Hogg, *Constitutional Law of Canada*, 2017 Student Edition (Toronto: Carswell, 2017), 3-2, n.5.

8. John T. Saywell, "Liberal Politics, Federal Policies, and the Lieutenant-Governor: Saskatchewan and Alberta, 1905," in *Historical Essays on the Prairie Provinces*, ed. Donald Swainson (Toronto: Macmillan, 1978), 188.

9. For greater detail on this debate, see D. Michael Jackson, *The Crown and Canadian Federalism* (Toronto: Dundurn, 2013); Christopher McCreery, "The Provincial Crown: The Lieutenant Governor's Expanding Role," in *Canada and the Crown: Essays on Constitutional Monarchy*, ed. D. Michael Jackson and Philippe Lagassé (Montreal & Kingston: McGill-Queen's University Press, 2013), 141–59; James McL. Hendry, *Memorandum on the Office of Lieutenant-Governor*

of a Province: Its Constitutional Character and Functions (Ottawa: Department of Justice, 1955); John T. Saywell, *The Office of Lieutenant Governor* (Toronto: University of Toronto Press, 1957; Copp Clark Pitman, 1986); and David E. Smith, *The Invisible Crown: The First Principle of the Canadian Government* (Toronto: University of Toronto Press, 1995; reprinted with a new preface by the author, 2013).

10. In the modern era, the governor general is appointed through a commission under the Great Seal of Canada, which is a general seal for Canadian government affairs under the control of the Canadian cabinet. The governor general is nonetheless still regarded as a personal representative of the Queen, despite the fact the appointment is no longer under the Sign Manual.

11. See section 58 of the *Constitution Act, 1867.*

12. Ontario's legislature was created as a unicameral body, with just a Legislative Assembly, while Quebec's legislature included both an appointed upper house (the Legislative Council) and an elected Legislative Assembly; see sections 69 and 71, respectively, of the *Constitution Act, 1867.*

13. *R. v. Amer*, [1877] UCQB 391 at 408.

14. *Lenoir v. Ritchie*, [1879] 3 S.C.R. 575.

15. Ibid., at 623.

16. Ibid., at 634.

17. *Mercer v. Attorney General of Canada*, [1881] 5 S.C.R. 538.

18. It should be noted that not all judges were of the same mind on these points, but the majority of judges hearing related cases clearly supported the subordination of the lieutenant governors.

19. *Proceedings of the Inter-Provincial Conference Held at the City of Quebec, From the 20th to the 28th October 1887 inclusively*, 29.

20. *Liquidators of the Maritime Bank of Canada v. The Receiver General of New Brunswick*, [1892] A.C. 437.

21. Ibid., at 441–42.

22. Ibid., at 443.

23. *Bonanza Creek Gold Mining Co. v. The King*, [1916] 1 A.C. 566.

24. In re *The Initiative and Referendum Act*, [1919] A.C. 935 at 942. The judges struck down provincial legislation to create a direct democracy

law-making power that bypassed the legislature and lieutenant govern-
or. If approved by a majority of voters, a referendum motion to repeal
legislation would take effect within thirty days of the clerk of the executive council having published the results in the provincial gazette. The
lieutenant governor's only role in a referendum that approved a new law
would have been to simply announce a date within thirty days of the
vote that the law was to come into effect. The Privy Council held that
the lieutenant governor's discretionary powers to grant or refuse royal
assent, and to reserve a bill for the federal cabinet's approval, would all
have been rendered meaningless in this new referendum process.

25. Ibid., at 943.
26. Reference re *The Power of the Governor General in Council to Disallow
Provincial Legislation and the Power of Reservation of a Lieutenant-
Governor of a Province*, [1938] S.C.R. 71 at 76.
27. Similar formulations are also used in British Columbia, Alberta,
Saskatchewan, Ontario, and New Brunswick.
28. The original phrase used in the legislation passed by the Nova Scotia
Legislature in its first sitting of 1758 was: "Be it enacted by his
Excellency the Governor, Council and Assembly and by the authority
of the Same has hereby Enacted ..." PEI's enacting phrase is: "Be it
enacted by the Lieutenant Governor and the Legislative Assembly of
the Province of Prince Edward Island as follows ..." Newfoundland
and Labrador legislation states: "Be it enacted by the Lieutenant-
Governor and House of Assembly in Legislative Session convened, as
follows ..."
29. It is instructive to note that the Quebec National Assembly now uses
the bare term "assent" while the website of the lieutenant governor
still refers to "royal assent"; see assnat.qc.ca/en/abc-assemblee
/projets-loi.html and lieutenant-gouverneur.qc.ca/roles-et-fonctions
/fonctions-en.asp. The Ontario legislature's website explains the reason for the term "royal assent": "This procedure is called Royal Assent
because the Lieutenant Governor is agreeing to the bill on behalf of
The Queen," ola.org/en/visit-learn/about-parliament
/legislative-process/how-does-a-bill-become-law-ontario.
30. *The King v. Caroll*, [1948] S.C.R. 126.

31. Ibid., at 130–31.
32. Paul Lordon, Jean Rhéaume, and Mary F. Macdonald, "The Structure of the Crown," in *Crown Law*, ed. Peter Lordon (Toronto: Butterworths, 1991), 29–33.
33. A lieutenant governor may write to the Queen directly for formal courtesies, such as congratulations on birthdays or anniversaries. Anything of substance, however, must be sent first to the secretary to the governor general.
34. Interesting examples of tours by members of the royal family to Saskatchewan can be found in Jackson, *The Crown and Canadian Federalism*, 168–73.
35. A majority in the Supreme Court of Canada held that this requirement was because "there is an international, a foreign relations aspect involved in the relationship of Canada and Great Britain…." *Reference re Resolution to Amend the Constitution of Canada*, [1980] 1 S.C.R. 753 at 820. This reasoning seems curious at best, since it was settled in 1930 that for all matters affecting domestic Canadian affairs the Queen must act on advice from Canadian ministers and not the British cabinet.
36. Government of Canada, "Honours and Salutes," updated October 24, 2018, canada.ca/en/canadian-heritage/services/protocol-guide-lines-special-event/honours-salutes.html.
37. The distinction dates to the early years of Confederation, when governors general were considered the only personal representatives of the monarch in Canada; "Excellency" is a term reserved for personal representatives of a sovereign. In Australia, state governors are addressed as "Your Excellency" along with the governor general, as they have always been regarded as personal representatives of the monarch. Foreign ambassadors are also addressed as "Your Excellency" in Canada, as they represent their head of state. For the Canadian government's guidelines, see Government of Canada, "Styles of Address," updated October 24, 2018, canada.ca/en/canadian-heritage/services/protocol-guidelines-special-event/styles-address.html.
38. Government of Canada, "Table of Precedence for Canada," July 3, 2015, updated October 24, 2018, canada.ca/en/canadian-heritage/services/protocol-guidelines-special-event/table-precedence-canada.html.

39. Government of Saskatchewan, "Table of Precedence,"saskatchewan
.ca/government/visual-identity-and-protocol/protocol-guidelines
/table-of-precedence.

40. Taken literally, this would mean that even in provincially organized events, federal cabinet ministers from Manitoba have a
higher ranking than provincial cabinet ministers. Government of
Manitoba, "Order of Precedence for Manitoba," gov.mb.ca/fpir/
protocol/precedence.html.

41. Government of Alberta, "Order of Precedence,"alberta.ca/protocol
-order-of-precedence.aspx; Government of New Brunswick, "Table of
Precedence for New Brunswick," updated February 2019, www2.gnb.
ca/content/gnb/en/departments/intergovernmental_affairs/protocol/
precedence.html; Government of Nova Scotia, "Table of Precedence,"
novascotia.ca/iga/tableprec.asp; Government of Ontario, "Ontario
Order of Precedence," updated July 18, 2019, ontario.ca/page/
international-relations-and-protocol#section-1. Prince Edward
Island makes no mention of members of the Privy Council, but
does mention Senators and MPs, who are ranked lower than
members of the legislature; Government of Prince Edward Island,
"Table of Precedence for Prince Edward Island," June 16, 2016,
princeedwardisland.ca/en/information/executive-council-office/
table-precedence-prince-edward-island.

42. Government of Quebec, "Ordre de préséance des autorités convo-
quées individuellement dans les cérémonies publiques organisées par
le gouvernement du Québec," May 2, 1990, mrif.gouv.qc.ca/content/
documents/fr/decret_577_90.pdf.

43. The current instructions were approved by order in council PC
1976-2593.

44. The rationale for this requirement was that the federal government
might have to appoint an administrator in the lieutenant governor's
absence. But since orders in council were passed to provide continuing authority for an administrator, some provinces have stopped
informing the federal minister. An example of the instructions issued
to a specific individual can be seen with the commission to appoint
Mayann Francis as Nova Scotia's lieutenant governor: PC 1976-2593,

nslegislature.ca/sites/default/files/demo/pdfs/0238_2006-09-00_
Commission.pdf.

45. Several provincial governments have closed the official residences
of their lieutenant governors. It is well known that the lieutenant
governors in Quebec have faced indifference and even hostility from
successive Quebec governments. During a dispute over the powers of
reservation, Alberta's Premier Aberhart went as far as turning off the
utilities in Government House to drive the lieutenant governor out
of his residence in 1937. See Alfred Thomas Neitsch, "A Tradition of
Vigilance: The Role of Lieutenant Governor in Alberta," *Canadian
Parliamentary Review* 30, no. 4 (2007): 19–28.

46. Kenneth Munro and Richard Toporoski, "Can the Queen Give Royal
Assent in a Provincial Legislature? A Debate Between Monarchists,"
Canadian Monarchist News 24 (Autumn–Winter 2005): 20.

47. Ibid., 17–19.

48. In *re The Initiative and Referendum Act*, [1919] A.C. 935 at 942.

49. It must be noted that there is one clear limit on the breadth of delega-
tion in the 1947 Letters Patent, with the power to amend the letters
patent being reserved to the monarch by Article XV. In addition,
there is some debate over whether the monarch's power to appoint a
new governor general is a power that must logically be retained by the
sovereign.

50. This distinction was underlined by the Supreme Court of Canada in
The King v. Caroll, [1948] S.C.R. 126 at 128–29.

51. The full text of Article II reads: "And We do hereby authorize and
empower Our Governor General, with the advice of Our Privy
Council for Canada or of any members thereof or individually, as the
case requires, to exercise all powers and authorities lawfully belonging to Us in respect of Canada, and for greater certainty but not so
as to restrict the generality of the foregoing to do and execute, in the
manner aforesaid, all things that may belong to his office and to the
trust We have reposed in him according to the several powers and
authorities granted or appointed him by virtue of the British North
America Acts, 1867 to 1946 and the powers and authorities hereinafter conferred in these Letters Patent and in such Commission as

may be issued to him under Our Great Seal of Canada and under such laws as are or may hereinafter be in force in Canada."

52. The Supreme Court of Canada has stated in other contexts that "Canada" may mean the "federal juristic unit" of Canada, the federal level of government. For example, see *Reference re Authority of Parliament in relation to the Upper House*, [1980] 1 S.C.R. 54 at 69–70, and *Reference re Resolution to Amend the Constitution of Canada*, [1981] 1 S.C.R. 753 at 825.

53. Jackson notes that there is already an informal practice in Quebec to address the lieutenant governor in French as "Excellence." He also reports that the 2004 meeting of lieutenant governors resulted in a request to the federal government for a change in the official protocol of address from "Your Honour" to "Excellency"; however, no change has resulted. Jackson, *The Crown and Canadian Federalism*, 188–89.

54. Section 58 of the *Constitution Act, 1867* says, "For each Province there shall be an Officer, styled the Lieutenant Governor, appointed by the Governor General in Council by Instrument under the Great Seal of Canada."

55. Jackson, *The Crown and Canadian Federalism*, 111.

56. *Royal Style and Titles Act*, [1985] R.S.C., c. R-12.

57. It should be mentioned that despite separate laws at the national and state level in Australia on royal style and titles, there remains an unresolved question as to their compatibility. See Twomey, *The Chameleon Crown*, chap.9.

58. Prime Minister Louis St. Laurent was clear when addressing the House of Commons during the passage of the style and titles legislation that it did not create a new office of Queen of Canada; see *Hansard* (February 3, 1953), 1566.

59. See Andrew Heard, "The Crown in Canada: Is There a Canadian Monarchy?" in *The Canadian Kingdom*, ed. D. Michael Jackson (Toronto: Dundurn, 2018), 113–32; and Smith, *The Invisible Crown*, chap. 3.

60. Jeffrey Simpson, *The Spoils of Power* (Toronto: HarperCollins, 1989), 309–10.

61. Jackson, *The Crown and Canadian Federalism*, 161–62.

62. Lise Thibault served as lieutenant governor of Quebec from 1997 to 2007. She was sentenced to eighteen months in jail and ordered to repay three hundred thousand dollars. *Thibault c. R.*, 2015 QCCQ 8910.

63. The three territories all have officials called commissioners, appointed by the federal cabinet, who fill most of these same roles as lieutenant governors and the governor general, despite not representing the Queen. They are needed because the territories all have legislatures based on the parliamentary system. By contrast, Canadian municipal governments are not organized on the parliamentary model, and therefore there is no official equivalent to the governors or commissioners.

64. For a discussion of the reserve powers and other constitutional roles, see Andrew Heard, *Canadian Constitutional Conventions*, chap.2; Jackson, *The Crown and Canadian Federalism*, 149–64; Frank MacKinnon, *The Crown in Canada* (Calgary: Glenbow-Alberta Institute/McClelland and Stewart West, 1976), chap.7; and Anne Twomey, *The Veiled Sceptre: Reserve Powers of Heads of State in Westminster Systems* (Cambridge: Cambridge University Press, 2018).

65. An order of appointment is given, starting with the chief justice of the province through other senior judges. Orders in council were passed for each province and are listed as PC 2017-2014 through 2017-2022 for all provinces except Newfoundland and Labrador, which is dealt with in PC 2018-0065. For an example, see the authorization for British Columbia, PC 2017-1715, at Government of Canada, updated April 31, 2017, orders-in-council.canada.ca/attachment .php?attach=35625&lang=en.

66. The federal government may have been precluded from including in these generic orders a mention of the administrator acting on the death of the lieutenant governor, because section 67 of the *Constitution Act, 1867* only authorizes the appointment of an administrator to act during the "absence, illness, or other inability" of the lieutenant governor. An argument could be made that "other inability" could be interpreted to include death; but only a court ruling could clarify that point.

67. Article VIII.

68. McCreery, "The Provincial Crown," 154.

69. For an account of these controversial events, see Andrew Heard, "British Columbia's 2017 Extraordinary Contribution to Constitutional Conventions," *Journal of Parliamentary and Political Law* 11 (2017): 563–70; and Robert Shaw and Richard Zussman, *A Matter of Confidence: The Inside Story of the Political Battle for BC* (Vancouver: Heritage House, 2018), chap.12.

70. Walter Bagehot, *The English Constitution* (Ithaca, NY: Cornell University Press, 1966), 111.

71. Jackson, *The Crown and Canadian Federalism*, 160–61.

72. See Jackson, *The Crown and Canadian Federalism*, 164–68; McCreery, "The Provincial Crown"; and MacKinnon, *The Crown in Canada*, chap.8.

73. Christopher McCreery, "Not the Governor General's Choice: Canadian Honours and the Butler-Pitfield Principles," *Journal of Parliamentary and Political Law* 13 (2019): 67n 34.

74. Steven W. Beattie, "Former Ontario Lieutenant Governor James Bartleman's Indigenous Summer Reading Camps Program Continues to Grow," *Quill & Quire*, December 13, 2018, quillandquire.com /omni/former-ontario-lieutenant-governor-james-bartlemans -indigenous-summer-reading-camps-program-continues-to-grow.

75. See BC Government House Foundation, "Programs," bcgovhousefoundation.ca/programs.

The Changing Role of the Governor General,

or How the Personality of the Office-Holder Is Changing the Perception of the Monarchy

Serge Joyal[*]

> Institutions will never be anything more than what their participants make of them. Everything depends on the wisdom of the political players and their ability to resist the illusions of power.
>
> — Marcel Gauchet

Introduction

The question is simple and straightforward: Have the twelve Canadians who have served as governor general since 1952 had an impact on the

---

[*] During his long career in federal politics, Senator Serge Joyal has worked with and observed nine governors general since 1971; as secretary of state, he was responsible for state protocol from 1982 to 1984.

public perception of the sovereign and the role the Queen plays under our Constitution? Finding the answer, which may not be simple or straightforward, will help us to understand how the office of the governor general has changed and adapted to remain relevant.

The governor general represents the Queen in carrying out constitutional duties and performing ceremonial tasks as the functional head of state on the Queen's behalf. During the present Queen's reign, there have been important developments with respect both to the perception of the Crown and to the governor general's relationship to it. These changes have occurred in step with Canada's continuing political, legal, and social advancement.

The question of the impact or relevance of the governor general's character arises at a time when an appreciation of the Crown includes a more abstract dimension in addition to the actual person of the Queen. This has become evident through the meaning attached to the act of swearing/affirming allegiance to the Queen required under section 128 of the Constitution or in becoming a citizen. According to a 2014 decision by the Ontario Court of Appeal,[1] the action of swearing or affirming an oath to the Queen no longer means swearing allegiance to the Queen as a person but to the symbol of the Crown that represents our form of government.[2] This recognition of the abstract meaning of the Crown is the result of historical evolution: it is not a matter of chance, but rather the result of successive political actions extending over more than a century that, taken together, have created a constitutional monarchy in Canada that is different and distinct from its original source.

Historical Perspective

The preamble to the *Constitution Act, 1867* states that Canada is "federally united into One Dominion under the Crown of the United Kingdom of Great Britain and Ireland, with a Constitution similar in Principle to that of the United Kingdom." The meaning of the preamble has changed significantly since Confederation as Canada gradually took steps to assert greater control over its own affairs, domestic and foreign. This process was pursued and eventually achieved without challenging the recognition and role of the Crown. The tipping point came with the First World War. Within the twelve years following the end of the war, Canada effectively obtained full independence and sovereignty. It started with the Treaty of Versailles of 1919, agreed to by Canada as a separate signatory — at its insistence; continued with the Balfour Report of the London Conference of 1926, when Britain confirmed its commitment to the equal status of the dominions within the Commonwealth; and was secured with the *Statute of Westminster* in 1931, by which the British parliament acknowledged in law the equality and independence of each nation within the Commonwealth, bound together through shared allegiance to the Crown.

Canada's continuing adherence to its constitutional monarchy was confirmed with the accession of Queen Elizabeth in 1952. In concert with several other Commonwealth nations, Canada adopted a *Royal Style and Titles Act* months before the coronation, which standardized the Queen's formal title, acknowledged her as the Head of the Commonwealth, and explicitly recognized her as Queen of Canada. Finally, when the Constitution was patriated in 1982, the office of the Queen was protected by requiring that any change or amendment to the office would require the unanimous support of the federal Parliament and each provincial legislature.[3] Given this reality, for the foreseeable future Canada will remain a constitutional monarchy, one that is modern and progressive, supporting the values and principles guaranteed by the Charter of Rights and Freedoms.

This history of constitutional development and growth is distinctly Canadian. The Supreme Court recently acknowledged that, through this process, Canada shifted from being a government of parliamentary supremacy to one of constitutional supremacy.[4] However, the fact that the Queen of Canada is the same person as the Queen of the United Kingdom creates a certain tension in the understanding of our system.[5] The position of the governor general and the appointment process related to it had a parallel development to that of Canada's quest for full nationhood. At the time of Confederation, the governor general served two functions: he was the traditional recipient of advice from the prime minister and exercised the Crown's prerogative right, in the words of Walter Bagehot, to be consulted, to encourage, and to warn; and he was also an agent of the British government, reporting to the colonial secretary on Canadian affairs.

In those early years, consideration in the appointment gave priority to British interests and the governors general were all men of distinguished public service who represented the political and social elite. In the first fifty years after Confederation, two of the governors general were members of the royal family: the Marquis of Lorne (1878–83), husband of the Princess Louise, a daughter of Queen Victoria, and HRH Prince Arthur, Duke of Connaught (1911–16), a son of Queen Victoria. After the war, an episode between the governor general and the prime minister had lasting implications for the office; this was the King-Byng affair, when a request by the prime minister to the governor general in 1926 for a dissolution of Parliament was refused. The fallout confirmed that the governor general is generally bound by the advice of the prime minister and can depart from it only in exceptional circumstances.

In addition, as of 1930, in keeping with the recognition of Canada's growing political maturity on the eve of the *Statute of Westminster*, London acknowledged the advisability of consulting the Canadian prime minister on the selection of the governor general, even though the candidate continued to come from the British elite.[6] From then on, the right of the prime minister to be consulted on the selection of a candidate was firmly established. The next step in the evolution of the office was to "Canadianize" the position of governor general by appointing Canadian citizens. This happened in 1952, the year before the *Royal Style and Titles Act* in 1953.[7] When Elizabeth II officially became the Queen of Canada, a title distinct from her title of Queen of the United Kingdom, her personal representative in Canada was for the first time a native-born Canadian.

The Canadian Governors General: Issues and Questions

The history of the office of the governor general helps to establish the political context for our assessment of how the personalities of the Canadian governors general since 1952 have exerted an impact on the perception Canadians have of the monarchy.[8] The key point is that these personalities have formed a kind of filter separating the role and the person of the monarch and contributing to the reduction of the Crown to a single abstract principle, while the ceremonial aspect has also acquired a lower public profile. Some pertinent issues arise.

First, certain facts have emerged gradually over the years and have had a definite impact on the public's perception of the governor general's role, which should be considered in a broader context to be fully appreciated.

The Queen does not reside in this country. In order to ensure a continuous exercise of the Queen's constitutional responsibilities, prerogatives, and symbolic attributions, Canada, as a constitutional monarchy, requires a governor general by default. This is not to say that the Queen or the royal family do not have historic ties and an abiding interest in Canada. During her reign, Her Majesty has made more than twenty-two official visits to Canada.[9] Canadians have always admired and been grateful for Her Majesty's consistent interest in and affection for Canada. Her father, King George VI, and her mother, Queen Elizabeth, were the first reigning monarchs to visit Canada. In 1939, they spent a month travelling across the country, from the east coast to the west (May 17 to June 15). From the late eighteenth century to the present, each generation of the royal family has had a particular link with Canada.[10]

However, the Queen has a presence and a role in British life that has no comparison in Canada. She is a central feature of society; the media continually scrutinize her activities and those of her family, and she remains at the core of Britain's historical identity. People of all nations identify with war, crises, and challenges that run through major stages of their history. In Great Britain, the sovereign stands at the epicentre of national life. This has no parallel in Canadian life, and such a role simply cannot be filled by the governor general.

It nevertheless remains important to consider the distinct and different impacts that the twelve Canadian governors general have had and the way in which their personality profiles have helped to shape Canadians' image and perception of the viceregal function, and consequently of the monarchy, inseparable from the people performing that role.

The first Canadian to fill the role of representing the Queen as head of state was Vincent Massey, a former senior diplomat, who served for seven years (1952–59). He and the eleven other Canadians have each added certain elements to the position of governor general — foremost of which is

King George VI and the Queen Consort Elizabeth appeared at the base of the Peace Tower during their tour of Canada from May 17 to June 15, 1939. This first visit by a reigning sovereign and his consort attracted large crowds. They received enthusiastic and cheering welcomes from east to west. Many souvenirs were produced to mark this unprecedented royal tour; among them were this mug and postcard of their visit to Ottawa. The production of such mementoes has been a standard feature of royal visits ever since.

the highly brief or transitory nature of their mandate — that have clearly influenced public perception of the role.

The hallmark of the Crown in a constitutional structure is to represent continuity and stability. In Britain, this has been exemplified by the long reign of the Queen, though in reality such continuity and stability really depend on knowing that the line of succession will pass on to her son, grandson, and great-grandson, her heirs and successors. In Canada this is not an option: there is a new governor general every five years on average. Queen Elizabeth represents stability and continuity, while the rapid succession of governors general in Canada maintains a permanent element of unpredictability. This is essentially the result of the exercise of the prerogative of selection by the prime minister, which also entails the prerogative to determine the term.

After Jules Léger (1974–79) served for a period of five years, then retired because of health issues,[11] Prime Minister Pierre Trudeau, who was in power at that time, decided the term of a governor general's mandate should be five years. Since then, the length of the governor general's mandate has been about five years. It has sometimes been extended for specific reasons,[12] for example, because the end of the governor general's mandate may have coincided with an election and constitutional certainty required that the governor general remain in office. In other words, extending the mandate beyond five years depends on the vagaries of politics rather than the term of the mandate. In reality, the prime minister's political needs dictate the length of the mandate of the governor general. Thus, the exercise of the privilege of the prime minister to select and recommend a candidate is linked with the power to determine the length of the term. Is five years enough? What are the implications of such a brief term?

A term of five years is equivalent to the duration of a Parliament, according to section 50 of the *Constitution Act, 1867* and section 4 of the Canadian Charter of Rights and Freedoms. It is curious that some officers of Parliament, such as the auditor general or chief electoral officer, are appointed for a full ten years and other officers for at least seven years in accordance with the legislation that enables their office, rather than being at the pleasure of the prime minister and his or her electoral interests. It is important to realize, too, that the terms served by many governors general have been far shorter than the average years of service of a member of Parliament (eight to nine years), not to mention the average ten or eleven years[13] served by senators that ensure the continuity and independence of the Senate's legislative function. With the Canadianization of the position of governor general, the prime minister controls the prerogative to select the candidate to be appointed by the Queen, to determine the term of the mandate and, at the limit, to recommend the dismissal of a governor general (one would hope that would happen only for a just cause, because the prime minister remains responsible for protecting the Crown and should certainly not appear to take an ill-thought-out or partisan decision).

Second, the prime minister's grip over the position of governor general is revealed in the type of person selected to be appointed governor general. Every prime minister since Louis St. Laurent who has served for at least one term (or two years) has chosen a candidate for this position.[14] What does the selection process reveal?

First and foremost, it reveals the principle of alternation between an English-speaking and a French-speaking governor general, thus reflecting the official status of equality of both languages in Canada. To this day, this criterion of selection is so intimately linked to the nature of our federal structure and Charter of Rights and Freedoms that any governor general should be able to communicate to Canadians in both official languages.

In reviewing the list of appointments, one realizes that the first eight Canadians who served as governor general had careers that fell into the more traditional category. They tended to be older persons[15] who had distinguished themselves in the diplomatic service, military, or politics and had served their country in high-level positions such as ambassador, army general, premier, senior federal minister, or university chancellor. They were accustomed to the strict framework of diplomacy, military discipline, or cabinet solidarity, and respected the hierarchy, rules, and practices that are part of high-level public responsibility. In general, they were men in their sixties who were nearing the end of their careers, aside from former Manitoba premier Edward Schreyer, who was appointed at age forty-four.

They retired quietly at the end of their terms and were rarely in the public spotlight afterward. The exception was Mr. Schreyer, appointed governor general in 1984. At the end of his five-year mandate he became

Canada's high commissioner to Australia and later even attempted a return to politics.[16] The majority of former governors general, however, have avoided the public eye or controversy,[17] thereby supporting the perception that the governor general does not get involved in divisive issues, avoids the appearance of having used the position for subsequent personal gain, and maintains the neutrality that befits the sovereign's constitutional responsibilities and the public's confidence and respect.

A shift happened when the first women were appointed, opening the position of governor general to reflect the developing social values of Canadian society. New social expectations emerged in the 1980s, among them the equality of women and men. Where it had once been advisable to appoint diplomats and experienced civil servants, greater emphasis began to be placed on choosing candidates who reflected the emancipation of women, new role models for ethnic diversity, unconventional professional occupations, and eventually Indigenous ancestry. No doubt the social and cultural values underlying the Charter of Rights and Freedoms had an influence on the selection of candidates to be recommended to the Queen, thus reflecting the evolution of Canadian society itself.

Four women have been appointed as governor general since 1984: Jeanne Sauvé, the first among them, was a Radio-Canada television journalist and host for many years, later a cabinet minister (1972–79) and speaker of the House of Commons (1980–84) — her political career was along the traditional line of the men who had previously served in that function; Adrienne Clarkson,[18] a well-known journalist on CBC television and later the agent general for Ontario in Paris; Michaëlle Jean,[19] who began her career in 1988 as a journalist on the public broadcasting system; and, most recently, Julie Payette, an astronaut until 2010, when she became a motivational speaker in demand in the private sector.

During their previous careers, these women were all in the news regularly or had maintained a public profile for several years. They shared common experiences: they had remained in the public eye during their careers, they were trusted figures in communications, and they were familiar television and media personalities. Jeanne Sauvé (sixty-two)[20] and Adrienne Clarkson (sixty) were appointed at the end of their careers, while Michaëlle Jean and Julie Payette were appointed at a fairly young age, forty-eight and fifty-three respectively, which normally means that people at the height of their career can move on to a next stage of their professional life once their brief five-year term as governor general is over.

One can hardly help noticing that these governors general received more media coverage and public attention because they had been popular, visible figures. All were skilled communicators, they were easily recognizable from their time on television, and they usually did not hesitate to take advantage of this to promote their message, their presence, and even their charisma, their unique personality traits, and their specific interests. In short, they are what popular culture calls "celebrities." The media know them well, and they can also use the media to their advantage. However, there is another side to the coin: they are more open to media criticism because they come from that "milieu" and their "star" status means that the specialized press follows them closely. The office of the governor general affords them a privileged platform to use their talents, confidence, communication skills, and, it must be said, their disarming charm to promote Canadian values that they hold themselves. And why not, one might ask, if this helps them communicate messages to the public as required of a governor general. Does not the position benefit in some measure from this fame and visibility? But these benefits are not without pitfalls.

One may well ask the following questions.

If these public figures, who have been familiar to and well-liked by a segment of the population for a long time, receive such heavy media attention, is there not also a risk that their dominant public image might have an impact on their function beyond the institution they have the mandate to personify? More broadly, when selecting a candidate for the position of governor general, can the prime minister disregard the impact of that person's previous career and personal history? Is the personality of the selected candidate not in fact a statement of the "message" that the prime minister intends to convey to Canadians? Candidates who have taken a stance or have been in situations in the past that generated debate cannot erase these after their appointment, and their previous career may also influence some people's perception of their performance of the viceregal duties. In addition, if the same exercise of selection happens every five years as a new person takes office, there may be reason to consider the longer-term impact of Canadians' perception of the viceregal position and ultimately of the role of the Crown itself.

Does this mean that one should exclude from the position anyone who has had a high-profile profession or was a prominent media figure, to avoid creating a grey area between the person of the Queen, who holds constitutional powers and carefully steers clear of any debate, and that of her Canadian representative, whose public image may be just as significant during their brief five-year term?

And, ultimately, is there not a greater risk that the prime minister could be annoyed by a governor general's media notoriety and feel the need to maintain close attention to them, especially if that prime minister did not personally select the person for the position? Because, with the exercise by the prime minister of the prerogative to recommend a candidate, comes also the constitutional responsibility to protect the Crown and the perception of it. There was a welcome initiative by Prime Minister Stephen Harper in 2010 to appoint a consultative committee to analyze and vet potential candidates — a process designed to minimize the risk of selecting a personality that could later reveal its limits.

Moreover, by appointing relatively middle-aged public figures as governors general, are we not inevitably changing this position into a welcoming step for career advancement once the brief mandate is over, and in so doing, are we not creating ambiguity about the objectivity that has consistently characterized a monarch's reign? Are we not, in fact, making the person serving as governor general more dependent on the government of the day for their subsequent career?[21] In short, are we not putting even more power in the hands of the prime minister, an irreversible trend that subtly weakens the balance of power in our system of government? Does the prime minister not end up finally controlling the very credibility of the governor general and the symbol they personify?

In the end, where does the essential nature of the sovereign's function really lie? The Crown guarantees continuity, stability, and political restraint, and holds the key to the principle of responsible government that is at the very heart of our constitutional democracy. Do we not obscure the basic role of the monarch by constantly and frequently changing the persons serving as governor general? Are we indirectly lowering the visibility of the

The Queen is the font of all honours, and the Order of Canada, created in 1967 to recognize outstanding service to the country, is awarded to distinguished Canadians in her name. The Order of Canada was established by statute and among its provisions is the advisory council that has the mandate to recommend candidates to the Order. The governor general serves as the chancellor of the order and, to ensure the impartiality and independence of the selection process, does not take part in the deliberations of the advisory council. In this photograph, the Queen proudly wears the Canadian insignia as Sovereign of the Order of Canada, and below it the Order of Military Merit. The photograph was taken in 1995 and reproduced on a commemorative plate celebrating her Golden Jubilee in 2002.

sovereign in favour of high-profile but essentially transitory figures who can use this function as a unique opportunity to develop a personal agenda that no longer takes shape at the end of their mandate but perhaps immediately after investiture?

Third, the prime minister's involvement in the governor general's future activities continues beyond the term of office.

It has long been the hallmark of many governors general to brand their office with particular initiatives that remain attached to their name: the Stanley Cup for men's hockey teams since 1892, the Grey Cup for Canadian football since 1909, the Clarkson Cup for female hockey teams since 2006, the Governor General's Performing Arts Awards, and the list goes on. It is, in a way, analogous to the various charities or causes supported by the members of the royal family. For instance, the Prince's Trust Canada[22] is well appreciated for its contribution to the improvement of the social and economic conditions of Canadians.

But an issue appears once the governor general has completed their term. Some have established foundations wherein they continue to pursue specific objectives. For instance, the Jeanne Sauvé Foundation for youth leadership, established at the end of her term with public and private money; the Institute for Canadian Citizenship established by Adrienne Clarkson; and the Rideau Hall Foundation for leadership and innovation established in 2017 by David Johnston. Those initiatives maintain the profile of former governors general in the public eye. Once the governor general has left office, controversy may arise over the public treasury's financial responsibility for their personal activities. The former incumbents remain leading public figures. They continue to be solicited by the communities they identified with during their term and the social or cultural causes they supported. Former governors general have access to public funds that are made available annually to assist them in their personal activities, which encourages them to pursue their cherished objectives and in turn invites the public to continue to solicit them.

A controversy arose in 2018 over the use of public funds to reimburse the annual expenses of former governors general some ten years after the end of their term, and over the issue of transparency,[23] showing that this situation cannot be ignored. Not taking into account the impact that the previous and future activities of office holders may have on the perception of the role of the monarchy and Canadians' reaction to it is fraught with ambiguity. A person who has held the viceregal office will always be in the public eye.[24] If they are publicly criticized, for whatever reason, justified or not, they may not be able to rely on the current prime minister to defend them,[25] since the person who recommended them to the sovereign may have left long ago and the successor may feel only slight responsibility now, leaving the former governors general mainly to fend for themselves in the public arena.

Canadians' perception of the role of the governor general and the monarchy is not changing just through laws and regulations. It is changing just as much through the social and cultural values they hold, as well as through the personality, public presence, and personal activities of the office holders, however legitimate they may be, and the commitments they continue to make after their term ends.[26] As long as public money is involved in the course of these activities, the prime minister, who has the responsibility to protect the Crown and the public purse, remains accountable for those decisions. This exposes the office of the governor general to continuous pressure and does not always increase its prestige.

Fourth, there has been a trend to limiting the public constitutional role of the governor general.

We are witnessing recent prime ministers taking subtle, slow, and progressive control of some of the sovereign's attributes and prerogatives. From December 4, 2015, to the autumn of 2019, there was only one throne speech in the Senate in which the governor general was able to remind Canadians that, in our constitutional system, legislative power is held by the sovereign. In London, parliamentary practice requires that a throne speech be delivered each year, regularly bringing the sovereign back to Parliament, dressed in royal symbols and accompanied by all the pomp of the monarchy. In the eyes of the British, the Queen is an integral part of Parliament and the constitutional concept of the "Crown in Parliament" is an immutable reality. Moreover, a large part of the Palace of Westminster, where Parliament sits, is the sovereign's personal property! The more the sovereign is seen as performing a well-defined constitutional function in London, in all her regalia, and exerting real influence, the less her Canadian representative can be seen as having comparable prestige. Since the 1990s there has been no grand opening of a new parliament with the diplomatic corps. Moreover, the prorogation speech by the governor general that used to be delivered in the Senate Chamber has been simply abandoned.

In Canada since 2002, royal assent to bills is given publicly in the Senate by the governor general at least twice each calendar year.[27] This change was initiated to address the situation whereby, in the absence of the governor general, justices of the Supreme Court were called to give assent to bills, some of which might eventually be challenged in the courts.[28] Now, in the governor general's absence, this responsibility is relegated to the executive secretary, or even to the deputy executive secretary, gutting it of all its symbolic importance and reducing this power to a mere administrative act. Having been relieved of some of the symbolic gestures that give this position its constitutional purpose, governors general compensate by taking an interest in personal causes, while their constitutional function stagnates and, to a point, slowly fades.

Unlike the Queen, who throughout her reign has received regular visits by the British prime minister and the daily royal "red boxes" informing her of important government decisions, and has relied on able and experienced advisors who are always at hand to assist her in her constitutional responsibilities, the governor general does not have the prerogative to be consulted, to encourage, or to warn the prime minister about government affairs. This takes away from the governor general the moral authority that the sovereign exercises in Westminster over "her" prime minister. The Canadian prime minister may consult with the governor general on occasion, but this courtesy is in no way comparable to the rigorously respected convention at Buckingham Palace. The governor general remains responsible for signing executive orders in council that are regularly sent to him or her, but this is not a visible part of their responsibility and is not seen by the public as fulfilling an essential role.

One should recall the failed attempt of Bill C-60, introduced in 1978, to raise the governor general's status to "First Canadian"[29] and the subsequent controversy over the governor general's status as head of state.[30] In terms of the sovereign's constitutional powers, this change was not just semantics. It went to the heart of our understanding of our system of government. The concepts of form and function cannot remain ambiguous without undermining the fundamental principles that are the only real guarantees of the stability of our system of government, without which, ultimately, Canada would be a constitutional monarchy in name only. We would lose all of the benefits of constitutional monarchy and leave the prime minister free to assume most of the prerogatives. The prime minister has been shown on the Government of Canada website inspecting guards of honour, when it is the governor general who holds the prerogatives of commander-in-chief, as stated in the Letters Patent, 1947.[31] No one, apparently, saw this as a usurpation of the governor general's constitutional responsibilities. The media remained silent.

As Head of the Commonwealth, the Queen has attended all but two of the twenty-five biennial Commonwealth Heads of Government Meetings (CHOGM) since 1971.[32] As sovereign of the United Kingdom, she has met with many international heads of state. The Canadian governor general has had no comparable international exposure. Since Governor General Roland Michener's first international trip on Canada's behalf, governors general have travelled and represented Canada abroad, but essentially to serve international political objectives defined by the prime minister; moreover, such trips remain rare.

There is a dynamic in our Westminster-style parliamentary systems that one cannot ignore: the prime minister is the head of government and tends to be seen as the effective head of state, or at least its surrogate. Presidents of foreign countries speak, meet, and agree to solve pending issues with the Canadian prime minister. In the eyes of the Canadian public, the prime minister carries the responsibilities of government; the governor general's prestige or leadership is not the umbrella under which Canada and its partner countries strive toward common goals. There is a subtle influence of a presidential tone in that dynamic. In reality, the office of the prime minister has displaced the principle that the Queen or the governor general exercises executive responsibility, as provided for in section 9 of the *Constitution Act, 1867*.

On the whole, what the sovereign loses in terms of prerogative, another power assumes. Power does not disappear when it changes locus; instead, it is usually absorbed by an entity that already holds power. It is wrong to believe that the place and role of the Crown are diminishing because of obsolescence; in other words, because they are no longer useful or important. The Crown represents a power. This shift in power is not necessarily beneficial to the democratic balance.

Fifth, it is important to note that the candidate that the prime minister selects as governor general may not have had the training or experience in their previous career that would have prepared them to master the arcane subtleties of their constitutional duties and to carry out a demanding role in terms of protocol and ceremonial symbolism.

Unlike members of the royal family, who are trained early in the protocol and ceremony of the office and the institution of the monarchy, the Canadian appointed to this position must learn all about the institutional principles that define this office and the requirements inherent in a responsibility that basically consists of exercising the powers and attributes of the sovereign. Put simply, no school curriculum can prepare someone for this symbolic high office. The person appointed governor general has to rely on experienced advisors at Rideau Hall. They are the ones who can guide the new governor general in a role and an institution that this person probably knew little about before being recommended to the sovereign by the prime minister.

The prime minister therefore makes a strategic choice in selecting someone with no experience in the institutions and principles of government, but rather for the social and cultural values they embody. No matter how brilliant or successful the candidate's previous career may have been, if they do not have the benefit of substantial diplomatic, military, or senior public service experience, they will have to learn everything. Having experienced advisors in place on the arrival of a new governor general facilitates the learning process and avoids many pitfalls. If these advisors leave with the outgoing governor general, real difficulties may quickly appear and the new incumbent could face serious difficulties, even with the best of intentions.

The lack of experienced advisors can make it very difficult for a new governor general to learn the role quickly. The exercise of the viceregal function is based largely on practices and conventions transmitted through the knowledge and mastery of the immediate advisors and their institutional memory, since governors general come and go. Once a governor

The Canadian governors general (left to right, top to bottom):

The Rt. Hon. Vincent Massey (1952–59)

Major General the Rt. Hon. Georges-Philéas Vanier (1959–67)

The Rt. Hon. Roland Michener (1967–74)

The Rt. Hon. Jules Léger (1974–79)

The Rt. Hon. Edward Richard Schreyer (1979–84)

The Rt. Hon. Jeanne Sauvé (1984–90)

The Rt. Hon. Ramon John Hnatyshyn (1990–95)

The Rt. Hon. Roméo LeBlanc (1995–99)

The Rt. Hon. Adrienne Clarkson (1999–2005)

The Rt. Hon. Michaëlle Jean (2005–10)

The Rt. Hon. David Johnston (2010–17)

The Rt. Hon. Julie Payette (2017–)

general manages to really master the position's requirements, it is almost time to leave the function. This lack of institutional knowledge can be all the more serious in situations of a minority government. An ill-prepared governor general could face serious political turbulence. Canada has not lived through many minority governments since 1952, but when it does, the system must have effective institutional safeguards. The prime ministers cannot ignore the constitutional responsibility of the governor general in such circumstances.

Sixth, the prime minister's initiative of modernizing the office of the governor general has remained willfully vague, paying little attention to protocol and state ceremonial.

The prime minister's desire to revitalize or modernize the office of the governor general, as expressed when announcing the appointment of Governor General Julie Payette in 2017, was a challenging objective. The governor general was left to take initiatives and then to explain herself. Neither the prime minister nor any minister of the Crown came forward to support her initiatives, and she gave personal interviews to answer the critics.[33] This is a situation that the sovereign never experiences; the Queen always shows considerable restraint and avoids controversy to preserve the dignity of the office. In the age of social media, public opinion can be unleashed without restraint or regard for decency, putting every person's reputation or office increasingly at risk; pushing "modernization" of such a secular institution is an initiative that has to be monitored with great care.

In fact, who is responsible for determining how to revitalize or modernize the governor general's role? Is it the governor general, on his or her own initiative? Why has the Privy Council remained so distant and not provided the expertise required to maintain this institution, which is essential to the functioning of our system of government?[34] The resulting dysfunction would lie with those who are responsible for maintaining the credibility of the system and ensuring its orderly operation; ultimately, it is the prime minister's responsibility.

What expertise is needed to conduct the delicate operation of modernizing a secular institution? In 2017, senior advisors at Rideau Hall left at the end of the previous governor general's term. The new incumbent had the best of intentions: she felt her objectives were valid, given what she had been led to believe about the nature of her particular mandate at the time of her appointment.

It must be recognized that this highly symbolic office, the holder of which is the personal representative of the sovereign and exercises her constitutional powers and attributes, must be assumed in a rigorous, dignified, and thoughtful manner. Any controversy over the governor general's personality and decisions is likely to have an immediate impact on the projected image, the perception of the role and the exercise of its related responsibilities, and lastly, on the convictions that Canadians generally hold about the monarchy. Canada's system of constitutional monarchy is a delicate balance; it cannot be fiddled with without risk to its stability and to the respect and trust Canadians place in it. One cannot engage in an improvised reform aimed at significantly changing the role of this office without having conducted an analysis of the nature of the office itself, which is the cornerstone of our democratic system. As one former governor general rightly wrote: "'The Crown is the ultimate expression of the legitimacy of our democracy.'"[35]

Before embarking on such a path, it is important to have a solid grasp of the country's constitutional history, an understanding of the principles that govern our parliamentary democracy, and a keen analysis of the ethics that guide the behaviour of the sovereign herself, who has occupied the throne in an absolutely remarkable and exemplary manner that a vast majority of Canadians across the country recognize wholeheartedly and admire sincerely. They expect the same from the person who represents her in Canada in all of her protocol and ceremonial responsibilities.

Rethinking the Office of Governor General

Serious thought is required before implementing initiatives that would move away from the previous role of the office and its practices, customs, and conventions that have stood the test of time. In the field of royal protocol, one must tread delicately, be careful, and avoid rushing: the Crown is a secular institution that has survived the vagaries of time and where each element, even a simple detail, has a meaning and importance for the orderly functioning and credibility of the whole. State ceremonial is an integral part of our system of government. It visibly expresses the "political" principles that underlie the machinery of government.

The governor general is a formal component essential to the functioning of the system; the role results from practices and conventions that have developed over long periods of our political history and, although they may appear secondary to some, they are central to the cohesion of our model of government, commanding respect by the majority and underpinning the common will to live together as free citizens in a constitutional democracy that is characterized by stability and historical evolution without major crisis.[36]

These practices and state ceremonial are intimately linked to the values we freely uphold. Altering or diminishing the respect due to the institutions that are entrenched in our history and define the government of Canada does nothing to strengthen the guarantee of our rights and freedoms. A system that falls apart, through recklessness or lack of knowledge of its inherent principles, will undermine the confidence of its citizens in its national identity.

The same applies to the symbolism of the person of the governor general, the representative mandated by Her Majesty to perform her constitutional duties and ceremonial role. As the governor general is at the top of the order of precedence in Canada, there is an expectation of dignity, rectitude, decorum, tact, and historical sense that define the very essence of the monarch's person. This dignity and rectitude, which are the primary qualities of the sovereign, require a certain restraint, an exemplary bearing, and a certain nobility of feelings, sensitivity, and respect for everyone. Governors general do not represent themselves, they essentially represent the sovereign: when expressing views, they are those of the Crown. In reality, does the sovereign's exemplary "professional" behaviour not define the parameters of her personal representative's conduct? Should not the Queen's irreproachable conduct in the exercise of her duties as sovereign inspire the approach of the person who receives Her Majesty's mandate to represent her personally? Of course, it is not a question of imitating the Queen, which would be ridiculous and ultimately a parody that would greatly discredit the office. However, as the French historian Marcel Gauchet argues: "Institutions will never be anything more than what their participants make of them.

Everything depends on the wisdom of the political players and their ability to resist the illusions of power."[37]

The question remains: To what extent can the personality and views of the person serving as governor general be superimposed onto the image of the sovereign and influence the performance of the Crown's responsibilities? When there are so few opportunities to publicly embody the sovereign's constitutional powers, are we not setting a trap for the governors general by encouraging them to glamorize the function, to take centre stage, or to promote their personal views and interests, however legitimate and good-hearted they may be? It seems that when one wants to engage in an exercise as complex as revitalizing or modernizing the highest office in the land, other than by simply appointing a younger candidate, albeit one with a remarkable and publicly admired career, it is wise to consider a number of preliminary conditions. Certainly, engaging in such reflection in a constitutional democracy like Canada is a laudable process, with the potential to generate positive effects. Institutions must be able to evolve according to contemporary needs and expectations, and it is the distinctive feature of British institutions and their resilience that they can adapt without shocks, upheavals, or tensions to the requirements of the times. This constitutes their innate genius and explains their survival through the centuries.

However, in the Canadian context this delicate exercise must be approached with careful thought and analysis. In the words of Michael Pitfield, a former senator and clerk of the Privy Council,[38] "In constitution-making it is important to bear in mind that the first step in reform is almost never the final step. To the contrary, the first step sets off a process of evolution usually quite rapid at first and gradually petering out. Focusing merely on the change and not on its consequences as far as the eye can see is to invite mistakes and chaos. Equally, it is important to build on the genius of the system itself ... to build on what exists, not on what is envisioned as ideal."[39] In other words, we must define the specific needs that this desire for revitalization or modernization seeks to address, along with the objectives pursued, taking care to respect the fundamental principles and essential character of a constitutional monarchy. In the words of experts on political systems, there is an "institutional grammar" to master before embarking on an exercise to rewrite the operation and functioning of such systems.

Are we not sinking into a form of "youthism," a fashionable movement rooted in "presentism," social concepts that are now popular and trendy? This mentality involves the tendency to decide on rapid changes to the institutions and conventions that form the foundation of our democratic system, without first gaining a historical perspective and assessing the immediate and longer-term impacts of their effect on the democratic system as a whole, which has so far ensured an incomparable level of freedom, equality, and unity in Canada. Nor is Canada a country without historical roots or important international presence. Many of the Western countries with which Canada has had a successful secular relationship are facing internal dysfunctions and divisions due to poorly thought-out initiatives. Let us learn from their experience and think seriously before we imagine that we can rewrite everything with a stroke of a pen.

Reforms that have constitutional impacts on the functioning of the entire system cannot be launched into the public domain without deep and sober reflection. It is easy to outline reforms that galvanize voters in an election platform, but implementing them requires an understanding and a great mastery of the institutional principles and the "internal architecture" of our system of government.[40] The political institutions that Canada has developed over 150 years are a complex combination of balance and counterbalance that should not be tinkered with simply to please voters or to ride on contemporary trends, and without consideration for the inconsistencies they may cause in the functioning of the system. Who wins in the end in this reorganization of power? The advantage of the monarchy is to keep political power in check and preserve a symbolic zone beyond which politics does not venture. If we take away all of monarchy's intrinsic qualities and keep only the word, who benefits if not the one who controls most of the system's strings? One has often seen this when legislative or procedural changes have been made in the past. They have never really diminished the prime minister's powers.

Selecting a candidate for governor general is a critical decision that requires wisdom and an intimate knowledge of the background of those who have held this position. It cannot be dictated solely by the criteria of fame or public esteem. In a way, the person embodies the values and ideals Canadians hope to have for themselves and that the Queen of Canada carries in her capacity as sovereign. The viceregal function is part of a whole that requires the simultaneous combination of several factors, each as essential as the other, to ensure its smooth performance.

Conclusion

In his 1995 book, *The Invisible Crown*, David Smith endeavoured to identify, down to the last detail, the subtleties of the monarchical principle that is distilled in the conventions and practices that have established a stable position for the office of governor general, an office that does not initially appear to require successive occupants to put a strong personal stamp on its exercise. The sovereign is the true holder of the constitutional powers recognized by the fundamental law, and for a very simple reason: it is the sovereign who, in the end, is the bulwark against a derailing of the parliamentary system.

Understanding the role of the person called upon to exercise the duties of governor general should be a prerequisite for selecting a candidate for the office. The candidate's personality (however endearing), their personal interests, their views, their status as a "celebrity" cannot be so dominant or glamorous as to call into question the neutrality that befits the sovereign and that she herself observes, and thus give more opportunity to the prime minister to take over the prerogatives. This would insidiously appropriate the monarchical reality without meeting the requirements of a real reform of our system of government. This is a risk that we should not take without a thorough reflection on its consequences for the future of our freedoms.

Perhaps one real and tangible reform, and an urgent one, is for the Privy Council to seriously consider how a more responsible selection process should be put in place. Prime Minister Justin Trudeau established two advisory boards in relation to public appointments of legislative and judicial importance: the Independent Advisory Board for Senate Appointments in January 2016, and the Independent Advisory Board for Supreme Court of Canada Judicial Appointments in August 2016. These boards clarified the selection criteria for candidates and rendered them more transparent; their establishment should be commended. However, in 2017 the prime minister abolished the advisory committee for the appointments of territorial commissioners, lieutenant governors, and governors general that had been established by his predecessor, Stephen Harper. There was no institutional reason for such a decision. Such a committee should again be formed to advise the prime minister on a list of potential candidates to be considered, conducting thoughtful analysis and employing a more clearly outlined set of criteria.

The Privy Council could help define the essential qualities that candidates should bring to the position of governor general, including among them criteria for assessing the appointee's personality, their merit, the social values they hold, and how they reflect on Canadian society, as well as how they may impact Canadians' perceptions of the benefits of our system of government. Moreover, there would be a clear institutional benefit for the objectivity and credibility of the function of governor general if the prime minister extended the term to a seven-year mandate. The perception that each prime minister can choose a candidate for a governor general's appointment runs contrary to the stability of the Crown. The idea that the function could be instrumentalized to serve the purposes of a prime minister jeopardizes the very neutrality of the Crown.[41]

The decision to select a candidate, whose personality meets a certain set of values, to be recommended to the Queen as governor general and the decision to determine their term of office are of primary importance. The monarchy remains at the heart of Canada's parliamentary democracy as it has harmoniously evolved for over 150 years. The Canadian citizen called to exercise the constitutional and ceremonial responsibilities of Her Majesty needs to give foremost priority to sustaining the enduring values that have made Canada the beacon of freedom that it is.

Notes

1. *McAteer v. Canada (Attorney General)*, 2014 ONCA 578: "allegiance to a symbol of our form of government in Canada" (para. 54); "as a symbolic commitment to our form of government and the unwritten constitutional principle of democracy" (para. 62).

2. Serge Joyal, "The Oath of Allegiance: A New Perspective," in *The Canadian Kingdom: 150 Years of Constitutional Monarchy*, ed. D. Michael Jackson (Toronto: Dundurn, 2018).

3. Section 41 of the *Constitution Act, 1982* provides for the amendment process to change the monarchical nature of Canada's political system.

4. *Reference re Supreme Court Act, 22. 5 and 6*, 2014 SCC 21, para. 89.

5. *Motard c. Canada (Procureure générale)*, 2016 QCCS 588.

6. Peter W. Hogg, *Constitutional Law of Canada*, 2nd ed. (Toronto: Carswell, 1985), 193. Lord Tweedsmuir was the first governor general (1935–40) appointed after the adoption of the *Statute of Westminster* in 1931. See J. William Galbraith, *John Buchan: Model Governor General* (Toronto: Dundurn, 2013).

7. *Royal Style and Titles Act*, SC 1952–53, c. 9.

8. Adrienne Clarkson, *Heart Matters: A Memoir* (Toronto: Viking Canada, 2006), 197.

9. "The Queen's 2010 tour marked her 22nd official tour of Canada as our Queen." Government of Canada, "Her Majesty Queen Elizabeth II," updated October 29, 2019, canada.ca/en/canadian-heritage/services/royal-family/queen.html. She first visited in 1951 when she was a princess.

10. Prince William, the future King William IV, served in the navy and was posted to Canada from 1786 to 1787; Queen Victoria's father, the Duke of Kent and Strathearn, performed military duties in Quebec City from 1791 to 1792, and in Halifax from 1790 to 1800; the Prince of Wales, the future Edward VII, came to Canada in 1860 to inaugurate the Victoria Bridge in Montreal; the Duke and Duchess of Cornwall and York, the future King George V and Queen Mary, made an official visit to Canada in 1901; the Prince of Wales, the future Edward VIII, owned a ranch in Alberta, which he acquired in 1919 and visited several times until 1941. The Queen's last visit was in 2010; since then the Prince of Wales has visited Canada in 2012, 2014, and 2017, the 150th anniversary of Canada's Confederation. Prince Andrew, Duke of York, attended school in Canada. Princess Anne, the Princess Royal, is patron of various Canadian organizations

and regiments. The Duke of Cambridge and the Duke of Sussex have visited Canada on various occasions.

11. Governor General Jules Léger suffered a stroke six months after assuming his duties. His wife, Gabrielle Léger, assisted him in his role until he retired.

12. Prime Minister Stephen Harper extended the mandate of Governor General David Johnston by two years, as his term came to an end close to the dissolution of Parliament and the 2015 federal election. Prime Minister Paul Martin extended the term of Adrienne Clarkson by a year.

13. Serge Joyal, ed., *Protecting Canadian Democracy: The Senate You Never Knew* (Montreal & Kingston: McGill-Queen's University Press, 2003), 323.

14. Except for Joe Clark, prime minister for ten months (June 1979– March 1980); John Turner, prime minister for three months (end of June to mid-September 1984); and Kim Campbell, prime minister for five months (June to November 1993).

15. Vincent Massey was appointed at age sixty-five, Georges Vanier at age seventy-one, Roland Michener at age sixty-seven, Jules Léger at age sixty-one, Edward Schreyer at age forty-four, Ramon Hnatyshyn at age fifty-six, Roméo Leblanc at age sixty-seven, and David Johnston at age sixty-nine.

16. In 2005, Mr. Schreyer ran as a federal NDP candidate in the Manitoba riding of Selkirk-Interlake, but was defeated.

17. Jules Léger died in 1980, one year after retiring from the position; Ramon Hnatyshyn died seven years later in 2002 after practising law out of the public eye with a major law firm; and Roméo Leblanc died ten years later in 2009, but health problems prevented him from having a high public profile.

18. Adrienne Clarkson is of Chinese (Hong Kong) ancestry; she immigrated to Canada in 1941 at the age of two.

19. Michaëlle Jean, Haitian-born of African descent and whose ancestors were slaves, immigrated to Canada in 1968 when she was eleven years old.

20. Jeanne Sauvé died in 1993, three years after leaving office, from an illness diagnosed several years earlier.

21. Michaëlle Jean was elected secretary-general of the Organisation internationale de la Francophonie (OIF) in November 2014 with the support of the Harper government; but at the end of her term, Prime Minister Justin Trudeau's government supported Louise Mushikiwabo, the candidate running against her, who was elected the new secretary-general in October of 2018. Also, in October 2018, David Johnston was appointed head of the Leaders' Debates Commission by the Trudeau government for the October 2019 federal election.

22. Prince's Trust Canada's website: princestrust.ca.

23. See the following newspaper articles about expenses incurred: La presse Canadienne, "Les dépenses de l'ex-gouverneure générale Adrienne Clarkson font sourciller," *La Presse*, October 31, 2018, lapresse .ca/actualites/politique/politique-canadienne/201810/31/01-5202496 -les-depenses-de-lex-gouverneure-generale-adrienne-clarkson-font -sourciller.php; Agence QMI, "Dépenses: «Je sers toujours le Canada», se défend Adrienne Clarkson," *Le Journal de Montreal*, November 3, 2018, journaldemontreal.com/2018/11/03/depenses-je -sers-toujours-le-canada-se-defend-adrienne-clarkson; "L'ex- gouverneure générale Adrienne Clarkson défend ses comptes de dépenses," *Radio-Canada*, November 2, 2018, ici.radio-canada.ca/ nouvelle/1133679/millions-dollars-reine-canada-depenses; or Brian Platt, "Expense program for former governors general has caused con- cern for two decades, Trudeau told in briefing note," *National Post*, July 29, 2019, nationalpost.com/news/politics/expense-program -for-former-governors-general-has-caused-concern-for-two-decades- trudeau-told-in-briefing-note.

24. Adrienne Clarkson, "I Am No Longer Governor-General but I Still Serve Canada," *Globe and Mail*, November 3, 2018, 08; "Set Limits for Their Expenses — Former Governor-General," *Toronto Star*, November 5, 2018, A10; Christie Blatchford, "Sure, Her Duties Are a Chore — But That's Not the Public's Problem," *National Post*, November 6, 2018, A4; Konrad Yakabuski, "Son Excellence," *Le Devoir*, November 3–4, 2018, B11; "Trudeau prêt à revoir les rè- gles de dépenses," *Le Journal de Montréal*, November 1, 2018, 14;

"Politique : l'ex gouverneure générale assure servir le Canada," *Le Journal de Montréal*, November 4, 2018, 8.

25. Clarkson, *Heart Matters*, 192–93.

26. Mélanie Marquis, "Débats des chefs — Bernier conteste la décision du commissaire," *La Presse*, August 14, 2019, lapresse.ca/actualites/politique/201908/13/01-5237254-maxime-bernier-reclame-sa-place-aux-debats-des-chefs.php.

27. *Royal Assent Act*, S.C. 2002, c. 15, art. 3 (1).

28. See Hugh Segal, "Royal Assent: A Time for Clarity," in *The Evolving Canadian Crown*, ed. Jennifer Smith and D. Michael Jackson. (Montreal & Kingston: McGill-Queen's University Press, 2012).

29. Bill C-60, introduced on June 20, 1978, section 44: "The Governor General of Canada shall have precedence as the First Canadian, and the office of the Governor General shall stand above and apart from any other public office in Canada." An Act to amend the constitution of Canada with respect to matters coming within the legislative authority of the Parliament of Canada, and to approve and authorize the taking of measures necessary for the amendment of the Constitution with respect to certain other matters, C-60, 3rd Session, 30th Parliament, Canada (1978).

30. Campbell Clark, "A Hot Debate About Head of State," *Globe and Mail*, October 10, 2009.

31. Letters Patent Constituting the Office of Governor General of Canada, effective October 1, 1947 — George R. See the Preamble, sections I and X.

32. The Commonwealth Heads of Government Meeting (CHOGM) is a biennial summit of the heads of government from all fifty-three Commonwealth nations; the Queen is head of state of sixteen of those member countries.

33. Brian Platt and Marie-Danielle Smith, "Julie Payette's first year as governor general: critics say turbulent, she says 'quite a ride!'" *National Post*, January 11, 2019; "Julie Payette a abordé l'adaptation à son rôle de gouverneure générale," *La Presse Canadienne*, September 27, 2018; Mia Rabson, "Julie Payette tente de rassurer ses employés," *La Presse Canadienne*, September 30, 2018; "GG Julie Payette — A

Year in Review / Une année en revue," general email from the Secretary of the Governor General (ggrsvp@gg.ca), October 2, 2018.

34. David E. Smith, *The Invisible Crown: The First Principle of Canadian Government* (Toronto: University of Toronto Press, 1995. Reprinted with a new preface by the author, 2013).

35. Clarkson, *Heart Matters*, 186.

36. The prorogation requested by Prime Minister Harper in 2008 and granted by Governor General Michaëlle Jean was recognized as having respected the practices prevailing in the circumstances. This situation did not alter the prestige of the Crown in any way. For more on this issue see Peter H. Russell and Lorne Sossin, eds., *Parliamentary Democracy in Crisis* (Toronto: University of Toronto Press, 2009).

37. Marcel Gauchet, "Je crains une anomie démocratique," Cercle des économistes, *Le Monde*, March 12, 2019, 2–3. [Translation.]

38. Clerk of the Privy Council 1975–79 and 1980–82.

39. Michael Pitfield, foreword to *Protecting Canadian Democracy: The Senate You Never Knew*, ed. Serge Joyal (Montreal & Kingston: McGill-Queen's University Press, 2003), xv.

40. Two examples illustrate this point: the changes to the electoral system proposed by Justin Trudeau's government in 2015, and subsequently abandoned; and the Senate reform supported by the Harper government, but ruled unconstitutional by the Supreme Court in 2014.

41. Clarkson, *Heart Matters*, 196–97.

A Tale of Two Secretaries:

Looking at the Roles of the Canadian Secretary to the Queen and the Secretary to the Governor General

Dale Smith

The offices of the Canadian secretary to the Queen and the secretary to the governor general play important roles in interfacing between the Crown and the government, in different capacities. But in recent years, the evolution of both offices has proven to be regressive in many regards. As we anticipate the changing face of the monarchy in Canada, where the current sovereign is unlikely to visit our shores again, how these institutions function will have increasing importance as the country navigates the road ahead.

In many respects, the office of secretary to the governor general is one of the oldest in Canada, going back as far as 1604, to the secretary to the governor of Acadia, Jean Ralluau. Ralluau served Pierre du Gua de Monts, and in the more than four centuries since, a secretary to the governor or governor general position has been in existence, performing both administrative and advisory functions.[1]

By contrast, the role of Canadian secretary to the Queen is a relatively recent construct, dating back to the 1959 royal tour, when the Queen decided that Lieutenant General Howard Graham, the tour's coordinator, should be styled as her Canadian secretary for the duration of the tour. The position was largely ad hoc until 1994, filled only when a tour was happening, and in some cases was patronage from the government of the day. In 1998, it was made an indeterminate appointment for the House of Commons' sergeant-at-arms, Major General Gus Cloutier, and was essentially a part-time position until Cloutier's death in 2005. A second indeterminate appointment was given to the Usher of the Black Rod in the Senate, Kevin MacLeod, in 2009, though MacLeod was named acting Canadian secretary in 2005.[2]

In 2012, MacLeod was named permanent Canadian secretary to the Queen as part of the Privy Council Office, until the change of government in 2015, when he was attached to the department of Canadian Heritage before his retirement in 2017. The post was vacant and "under review" by the government for nearly three years, while officials from Canadian Heritage handled the coordination of subsequent royal tours.[3] The former minister of Canadian heritage, Mélanie Joly, had anecdotally been known to tell people that she was the Canadian secretary while she was in office. In November 2019, the government appointed Donald Booth, director of strategic policy in the Machinery of Government branch of the Privy Council Office, to the position on a part-time basis.

Both positions play a conduit role to the Queen and the various royal households in London, but in different capacities. Whereas the secretary to the governor general is largely more concerned with issues of statecraft, the Canadian secretary to the Queen not only dealt with royal tours, but under MacLeod's tenure, among other things, proactively coordinated messages to Canada from the Queen for notable events, both in terms of celebration and condolences, even though the messages were issued by Government House.

Secretary to the Governor General

The secretary to the governor general, and the analogous private secretaries for the lieutenant governors in the provinces, has been described as a job with many roles to it — bureaucratic functionary, chief of staff, administrative head of the viceregal household and office, and the gatekeeper and guardian of access to the Queen's representative. In addition, the secretary also tends to serve as confidant, advisor, arbiter, and often friend, and has been called essential to the relationship between the viceregal and the head of government.[4]

The secretary to the governor general, in contrast to the provincial counterparts, also operated post-Confederation as an amalgamation of the roles of civil secretary, private secretary, and military secretary — the latter being a role that was separate until 1922, when the commander-in-chief role of the governor general was transformed into a symbolic and ceremonial post. While the civil secretary position began as one that was involved in the preparation of dispatches to the home country, and at one point headed up the administration of the original colony, after responsible government was achieved it returned to an advisory role to the governor. Post-Confederation, the position involved interface with Buckingham Palace, eventually the Canadian honours system, and more recently being the deputy of the governor general.[5]

The manual on the office, described as the Government House *Green Book*, written between 1931 and 1934 by the secretary to the governor general at the time, Alan Lascelles, described the position as not only holding the courtesy rank of deputy minister; the secretary had to also furnish the governor general with information and advice on any subject, and, if he could not, would have to know where to get the information. The secretary had to keep the governor general in touch with current events and public opinion, know the constitutional position of the viceregal office, its duties and limitations, act as a buffer between governor general and the less desirable aspects of the outside world, and ultimately be responsible for maintaining the proper traditions of Government House. The secretary was also responsible for the administration of the governor general's office; the submission of all state papers requiring the governor general's attention or signature; handling the governor general's correspondence, including invitations and the preparations that those invitations might entail; maintaining the lines of communication between Government House, Buckingham Palace, and the Prime Minister's Office; arranging formal meetings with the prime minister and other officials; arranging all formal and ceremonial functions; preparing materials for the governor general's speeches, messages, and replies to formal addresses; maintaining etiquette and precedence; administering the appointments of honorary aides-de-camp; administering the governor general's patronage; and arranging travel, official tours and visits, and relations with the press.[6]

In the time since the *Green Book* was written, there have been additions to the secretary's role: for example, its capacity as herald chancellor of the Canadian Heraldic Authority, which was created in 1988 when the governor general was authorized by letters patent to exercise the sovereign's powers related to heraldry in Canada. The office of the secretary expanded so that there was a department within Government House to deal with the administrative details of the various aspects of the job, including media relations. Currently the office is divided into three branches — "Policy, Program and Protocol," which organizes public events and visits, as well as the governor general and commander-in-chief programs in Canada and abroad; the "Chancellery of Honours," which administers the Canadian honours system, several Governor General's awards, and the Canadian Heraldic Authority; and the "Corporate Services" branch, which focuses on the administration and logistics of running Government House.[7]

Another signal of the importance of the secretary to the governor general was the fact that he or she was provided with an official residence, Rideau Cottage, on the grounds of Rideau Hall and within walking distance of the hall. Rideau Cottage, built between 1867 and 1868 and expanded in 1872, is described by the National Capital Commission as "a generously scaled, Georgian Revival brick house … It is a two-storey, hipped roof building with a bay wing on its northeastern façade. The building is distinguished by its symmetry, classically inspired doorway with pedimented porch, its sash windows and paired chimneys."[8] It was the home of either the secretary or the military attaché of the governor general until 2015, when it was decided that it would serve as the interim official residence of the prime minister while the National Capital Commission decided what to do about the crumbling 24 Sussex Drive.

There was a move from the practice where individual secretaries came into office along with their governors, to a period where a single secretary, Esmond Butler, served four successive governors general and Judith LaRocque served two.[9] For the majority of the post-Confederation life of the office, appointments were made from a pool of senior civil servants, but we are now back to a system where each governor general installs his or her own secretary, with little apparent regard for continuity or institutional memory.

The most recent governor general, Julie Payette, installed a long-time friend as her secretary, despite the fact that the person in question had no connections to the civil service or matters relating to the Crown before the appointment. An associate secretary position was created at the same time, staffed by a long-time bureaucrat from Canadian Heritage — a tacit acknowledgement that a working knowledge of the institutions of government is a requirement for the job and that if the person nominated by the governor general could not fulfill that role then a new position would need to be added to ensure that there was sufficient capacity in Government House. Around that time, much of the institutional knowledge left Government House, as many long-time staffers resigned, along with the departing secretary, citing frustration with the new occupants.[10]

This sort of regression to an earlier model of personal appointment should be a cause for concern when it comes to the role of the secretary to the governor general. This is because of changes made to the position in 2012, where the secretary was given the power to act as a deputy to the governor general and the ability to give royal assent to bills in written form (as opposed to the royal assent ceremonies that take place in the Senate Chamber twice a year) — a power that was previously reserved for a justice of the Supreme Court in his or her role as the deputy governor general.[11]

The fact that this much power and authority can be granted to someone who has no institutional knowledge or experience raises questions about how much value we place on having key people in place who understand our constitutional norms — particularly given some of the recent experiences in this country with government formation in hung parliaments, and discussions around possible coalition governments, as happened in 2008. Furthermore, Buckingham Palace relies on the secretary to the governor general for information about what is happening in Canada. If the person installed in the office is only there because of their personal relationship with the governor general, this raises the additional question about whom the palace can turn to if they do not have confidence in the secretary.

Canadian Secretary to the Queen

The decision to make the Canadian secretary to the Queen a permanent position was made in conjunction with the establishment of a viceregal appointments committee under the government of Prime Minister Stephen Harper as a way of "professionalizing" how viceregal representatives are chosen. The idea was first broached in 2010, when an ad hoc committee was struck to help search for a replacement for Governor General Michaëlle Jean. That committee, which included Kevin MacLeod, helped narrow down a short list of five candidates that would go on to Harper for eventual clearance procedures and selection, and led to the appointment of Dr. David Johnston as Jean's successor. Because of the relative success of that process, in 2015 Harper opted to make it a permanent process for the appointment of future lieutenant governors, territorial commissioners — even though they are not representatives of the Queen — and governors general. Upon the change in government in 2017, however, the committee was disbanded and the process remained "dormant" while the government considered its future role and mandate, according to government officials.[12]

MacLeod described the role of permanent Canadian secretary to the Queen as having four major components: to advise the prime minister and his government on matters that relate to the Crown in Canada, to have a direct involvement in national celebrations and commemorations, to chair the viceregal advisory committee, and to chair committees responsible for the delivery of all official royal tours in Canada. Of the four components, chairing the viceregal appointments committee took up the largest portion of his time.[13]

The advisory role of the office was less a constitutional one than it was about optics and media when it came to the Crown in Canada. After all, as most Canadians do not understand the role of the Crown, this advisory role was to help bring awareness to Canadians, not only by coordinating messages from the Queen, but also by distributing publications like *A Crown of Maples*, which MacLeod had produced for the department of Canadian Heritage in 2008 and updated in 2012 and 2015. There are now some 350,000 copies in circulation around the country.

Responsibility for the optics of the Crown in Canada was folded into the planning for royal tours, which is another way of strengthening the bonds of the Canadian Crown with the royal family by putting a face to the institution. As chair of the committee overseeing tours, MacLeod would develop the tour with the provinces and territories where the visit would take place, ensuring sufficient regional balance was present, and in coordination with those levels of government he would develop a "thematic" for the tour that would link to topical issues for Canadians, something MacLeod started when he was at Canadian Heritage coordinating royal tours in 2001. The thematic was a collaborative effort between the federal and provincial or territorial governments, as well as the chiefs of protocol in those provinces that would be visited during the tour. The advantage of using the thematic approach in the office of the Canadian secretary to the Queen, located in the Privy Council Office, was that a royal tour might involve as many as twenty-five different departments as well as different levels of government, each with its own vision and mandates. Having a centralized focal point that was not required to report to a department's deputy minister allowed for a more concise and concrete approach to royal tours, so that their impact was more readily seen by Canadians and resonated more strongly with them. Another of MacLeod's duties as secretary when it came to the preparation for royal tours was to draft speeches for the members of the royal family as well as the prime minister on the tour, which allowed for the thematic to carry forward in the messaging that emerged.[14]

Having the Canadian secretary role in the Privy Council Office allowed MacLeod to meet with premiers, lieutenant governors, and chiefs of protocol in developing the thematic. During the reconnaissance portion of planning, locations for the visits and the events they were marking could all tie into the thematic so that there was a consistent message — something most easily achieved by having the Canadian secretary layer in the structure. It also allowed for more forward planning of upcoming tours several years out, though the original five-year plans for tours had been curtailed, given the uncertainty around whether or not the Queen would travel to Canada again. Nevertheless, a master list of significant anniversaries that might warrant a royal tour was maintained and kept under active consideration at that point.[15]

The viceregal appointments were the largest part of the office's function: coordinating the committee that carried out the search for successors to fill upcoming vacancies among the lieutenant governors and territorial commissioners. While historically lieutenant governors had been patronage appointments, as they were considered delegates of the Dominion government, they eventually came to be overseen by the appointments secretariat within the Prime Minister's Office (PMO), around the time of the Mulroney government.[16]

Whereas the original ad hoc Governor General Expert Advisory Committee that Harper struck to formulate a list names for Jean's replacement included six members and garnered about three hundred CVs for the committee to narrow down to a short list of five names, the Advisory Committee on Viceregal Appointments that was created in 2012 consisted of three permanent federal members and two provincial or territorial members drawn from the province or territory in which a lieutenant governor or territorial commissioner was being nominated. They would typically receive about fifty CVs to draw down to a short list of five names to advance to the prime minister. The three federal members included MacLeod as Canadian secretary and chair of the committee and one anglophone member and one francophone member, both of whom who had extensive knowledge of the Crown and the role of the office.

The search period for a lieutenant governor or territorial commissioner in a given province or territory averaged about two to three months, with clear criteria spelled out for the members of the advisory committee as they contacted various groups and officials in that province or territory. Those criteria did include the directive that, while a person under consideration could have a political past, they would need to be seen as acceptable to all parties at present. Afterward, the committee would meet in Ottawa and go through the CVs they had received until the short list was drawn up for presentation to the prime minister. The short list was turned over in a face-to-face meeting with the prime minister, and that was where the committee's role ended — all vetting and screening was left to the Privy Council Office to arrange with the RCMP, the Canada Revenue Agency, and so on. The committee members deliberately did not want to know who the successful candidate would be until the name was announced by the prime minister.[17]

This separation is important, because accountability for such appointment rests with the prime minister, and enforcing that separation once the short list has been turned over ensured that the prime minister could not launder the appointment prerogative through the advisory committee. It also helped to keep the committee above partisan considerations.

The involvement in national celebrations and commemorations was probably best illustrated by MacLeod's spearheading the Diamond Jubilee celebrations in 2012, which included commissioning a new Canadian portrait of the Queen and the creation of the Diamond Jubilee medals. He worked with the Bank of Canada in 2015 for the twenty-dollar banknotes to commemorate the Queen's reign surpassing that of Queen Victoria to make her the longest-serving monarch in Canada's history. He also worked with the Royal Canadian Mint and Canada Post on the texts that accompanied commemorative coins or stamps, ensuring that they properly reflected that it was the Queen of Canada who was being commemorated.[18]

Another role that MacLeod took on as part of his duties as Canadian secretary was to coordinate the appointment of members of the royal family as colonels-in-chief (or their equivalent titles) in the Canadian Armed Forces and the RCMP. This involved not only all aspects of coordination that happened when a regiment stepped forward to request a colonel-in-chief, providing they had a strong rationale, but also involved the Canadian secretary proactively approaching regiments and making suggestions when there were important anniversaries upcoming for those regiments that might be marked by royal patronage, including the appointment of a colonel-in-chief if they did not already have one. This level of coordination involved unofficial conversations with the private secretaries in the households in London, depending on whether the regiment had a member of the royal family in mind, or whether they would have the Canadian secretary suggest one based on his knowledge of the members and their interests. This might also include whether any sister regiments in the United Kingdom had a member of the royal family already named as a colonel-in-chief and whether that might be extended to the Canadian regiment as well. If the private secretaries indicated that the member of the royal family was amenable, then the coordination involved putting forward the official paperwork through Government House.[19]

The program was expanded by MacLeod with the creation of the title of Commissioner-in-Chief of the RCMP for the Queen in 2012. The position had previously been dubbed "Honorary Commissioner," but that was felt to be inappropriate, as the Queen should not be honorary anything. He also saw to the creation of commodores-in-chief for the Royal Canadian Navy, patterned on the similarly created titles for the Royal Navy in 2006. MacLeod sought the approval of the Queen, the Prince of Wales, and the Princess Royal for the creation of Canadian commodores-in-chief, and, when it was granted, oversaw the nomination of the Prince of Wales as commodore-in-chief of Fleet Atlantic and the Princess Royal as commodore-in-chief of Fleet Pacific.[20]

Throughout this period MacLeod also worked with Government House and the Department of National Defence to create a formalized process for future colonel-in-chief requests, along with proper forms for submission. Similarly, MacLeod and his counterpart at Government House, Stephen Wallace, put into place a formalized process and forms for royal patronage and the designation "royal." MacLeod also proactively worked with groups to explain these honours, as most Canadians were unaware that they were available. To that end, he helped secure a royal designation for the Royal Aviation Museum of Western Canada in Winnipeg and the patronage of the Prince of Wales for the Willowbank School of Restorative Arts in Queenston, Ontario.[21]

As part of the Trudeau government's decision to "review" the office of Canadian secretary, a briefing note called on then minister of Canadian Heritage Mélanie Joly, to make a decision on the position before it became vacant, stating that there appeared to be no similar positions to it in other Commonwealth countries. It also noted that when the position was transferred to Canadian Heritage from the Privy Council Office its budget did not accompany it, which gives a clue as to how the government felt about the office, though when they did restore it three years later, they did so in the Privy Council Office as a part-time position.[22]

The new Canadian secretary, Booth, has stated that he largely views his position within the Privy Council Office as being one of a central point of contact between the Canadian government and the royal households, and is content to leave the planning for royal tours within Canadian Heritage. While Booth played a role in vice-regal appointments within his role in the Privy Council Office, he has stated that there have not been any indications as to whether or not the government will restore the viceregal appointments committee.[23]

Looking Forward

Given that the monarchy is in a time of transition in Canada, we should note that some of our viceregal institutions are showing signs that they, too, are in a period of transition, as the personalities of individual governors general have shown that some of what many Canadians have come to expect — such as the continued patronage roles for certain groups or awards — may not carry forward. At the same time, we have entered into a period where it is unlikely that the Queen will ever visit Canada again, and when we face the unfortunate demise of the current sovereign and the accession of her successor, he may be of an age where his travels to Canada will be limited, too.

It is also apparent that we will face challenges when that demise happens in terms of the agitation of republican forces within the country, be it from provincial actors in Quebec or the "progressives" that align with political parties like the NDP, whose party conventions have often included resolutions about abandoning the monarchy upon the death of the Queen. Of course, the reality in Canada is that any change to the status of the Crown, including the office of the Queen, requires a constitutional amendment unanimously agreed to by both Houses of Parliament and all ten provincial legislatures. This ensures that a republican option is a virtual impossibility. Consequently, we have the choice of treating the Canadian monarchy either as a historical curiosity or as a robust institution that has adapted to modern realities.

To that end, there should be a few adaptations to these two offices that reflect the path toward a more robust institution. With regard to the secretary to the governor general, we should encourage an approach in which secretaries have more continuity than being someone beholden to the personality of an individual governor general. It has been remarked that some of the more successful viceregal offices in the provinces have a private secretary who stays in office between eight and twelve years, in order to provide continuous and consistent advice for more than a single viceregal term and to train both the incumbent lieutenant governor and their successor — and their own private secretary successor. If this kind of thinking could be replicated within Government House in Ottawa, it would ensure that the pool of experience that a governor general can draw upon would be deeper than it currently is.

Because of the expanded powers of the secretary to the governor general, having more continuity would also be an asset because it helps to ensure more distance between the governor general and the secretary. While there is a debate in academic circles about drawing up a new Cabinet manual to help eliminate ambiguities around circumstances such as government formation in hung parliaments, or the establishment of formal or informal coalitions, I would remain somewhat cautious, because that would lessen the governor general's power of discretion, and would also diminish the secretary's advisory role to one of simply consulting the manual and hoping to find the situation sufficiently covered there.

I would see a role for a reinvigorated and permanent Canadian secretary to the Queen, and one that remains attached to the Privy Council Office, not to Canadian Heritage or even Government House, as has been suggested by some. The simple reason the office cannot be housed in Rideau Hall is that the Queen has eleven representatives in Canada, not just one. Being with the Privy Council Office allows the Canadian secretary the freedom to communicate with all eleven representatives on a number of issues, as well as to have more authority for dealing with federal departments at the deputy minister level, given that a royal tour can involve as many as twenty-five different departments. After all, a Canadian secretary should have a level of political astuteness that a mid-level bureaucrat at Canadian Heritage may not possess. A mid-level bureaucrat is more likely to be concerned with what the department is looking to achieve, as well as what the Prime Minister's Office is looking for — which would be less of a concern for a Canadian secretary under the Privy Council Office, as from there he or she has more direct access to either the prime minister or his or her chief of staff.

This renewed Canadian secretary position would also see the restoration of the viceregal appointments committee. Its demise made little sense, given that the Liberal government largely replicated its essential characteristics when it created its Senate appointments advisory committee, and to a more limited extent, the advisory committee for the appointment of justices to the Supreme Court of Canada. Over the course of its short lifespan, the viceregal appointments committee certainly appeared to most observers to prove its worth. It ensured that there was a robust and professional process that guaranteed adequate outreach at arm's length from the Prime Minister's Office, and that wound up ensuring a good gender balance of nominated candidates — more than most of the other appointment processes at the time. It also was seen by those provinces and territories to offer them more ownership of the process because of the buy-in that the consultations provided them.

As well, given the fact that two lieutenant governors died in office in the summer of 2019, having the appointments committee in place would provide reassurance that there were plans in the works for the swift replacement of the lieutenant governors before their respective provinces reached the point of paralysis. They would have short lists on file, or have already been engaged in the work of searching for a replacement if the affected lieutenant governor was already near the end of their term or was terminally ill, as was the case with the Saskatchewan and New Brunswick lieutenant governors in 2019.

There would also be room for a shift on the royal patronage front with a renewal of the role of the Canadian secretary to the Queen. As Rideau Hall appears to be moving away from the more robust patronage model that had grown up over the past several decades, it creates an opening for some of that patronage to come under the auspices of members of the royal family. A Canadian secretary who can proactively work with groups in Canada to seek patronage or a royal designation and communicate with the households in London and their private secretaries would better be able both to advise the royal households on the applicants in Canada and to assist with the coordination of that patronage role. This would not have any effect on the secretary to the governor general's role in communicating with Buckingham Palace on matters of state, but would simply spread that workload around more effectively.

To that end, there is great utility in having the Canadian secretary playing a more active role in dealing with the private or working visits of members of the royal family, which already take place and could take place more frequently if their patronage role in Canada was boosted — something that may be worth capitalizing on, given the family connections of Camilla, Duchess of Cornwall, to Canada (one of her ancestors, Sir Allan Napier MacNab, was a pre-Confederation premier in the Province of Canada between 1854 and 1856), and the connections that Meghan, Duchess of Sussex, forged in Toronto when she worked there as an actress.

Working visits could entail more support from the federal government. There could even be a small pot of money that the provinces hosting the working visits would be able to draw from; this would give the federal government more visibility, though it has also been noted that care should be taken to avoid giving the impression that the federal government is bankrolling the working tour. This more active role for the Canadian secretary could also create an outlet for advice from the Canadian secretary to private secretaries to the lieutenant governors and provincial chiefs of protocol. That would also allow for continuity of advice that we may not be getting if we continue along the path of secretaries to the governor general being personal appointments who do not have a grounding in the machinery of government or the workings of the Crown in Canada.

Another reason this conduit for advice is important is that there may not always be a harmonious working relationship between the secretary to the governor general and the Canadian secretary to the Queen. It is generally understood that MacLeod and Wallace got along well together, would even brief new lieutenant governors together, and would work together on some proactive measures, such as the declaration of loyalty to the Queen from the lieutenant governors and territorial commissioners for the Diamond Jubilee in 2012 and again in 2013 for the sixtieth anniversary of the coronation. Nevertheless, problematic appointments to the post of secretary to the governor general mean that having that additional place for advice would be a boon during times where there is a less amenable atmosphere in Government House.

There are important commemorations that a renewed, permanent Canadian secretary should start planning for, which include the Platinum Jubilee on February 6, 2022, as well as May 27, 2024, when Queen Elizabeth II will surpass Louis XIV as the longest-reigning sovereign ever. Current indications are that the new Canadian secretary considers the Diamond Jubilee to be one of the projects by which the office was made permanent at the time, but the secretary has not made any indications about plans for these future commemorations.[24] There is also the opportunity for greater outreach for the educational component of the position, beyond the distribution of *A Crown of Maples*.

We cannot also forget the preparations that the government should be making around the eventual demise of the current sovereign and the importance of having a Canadian secretary in place as part of that transition plan. While much of the work will likely be done by the clerk or deputy clerk of the Privy Council at the time, there should be a public face to what needs to happen in Canada. This should be someone who not only carries more weight with the public than a senior bureaucrat does, but has more *gravitas* to fend off the troublemakers that will try to capitalize on the event to push a republican agenda. The Canadian secretary will likely be in a better position for this than certain academics who might otherwise have to be relied on to do the heavy lifting.

I believe there is an opportunity for the government to create something unique within the Commonwealth. The creation of a permanent full-time Canadian secretary role within Privy Council Office has the potential to depoliticize the monarchy, which was an unfortunate side effect of the way in which the Harper government went about their program of renewing some of our monarchical links. Not getting sufficient buy-in from opposition parties, and justifying it as being about our history rather than stressing that Canada is a constitutional monarchy and it behoves us to act like one, allowed the media to carry the narrative that this was about attempts to glorify our colonial past rather than to reinvigorate the Canadian monarchy in the present. A permanent full-time office would signal that this is not the project of a single government, but one that crosses partisan lines, and that the Canadian monarchy is not the project of a single party. It would demonstrate that Canada, even if it is unique in the Commonwealth, can reinvigorate our relationship with the Crown and take the next steps in the evolution of the Canadian monarchy into something than serves our country in a better and more robust way than what we have currently.

Notes

1. Christopher McCreery, "Confidant and Chief of Staff: The Governor's Secretary," in *Canada and the Crown: Essays on Constitutional Monarchy*, ed. D. Michael Jackson and Philippe Lagassé (Montreal & Kingston: McGill-Queen's University Press, 2013).
2. Ibid.
3. Dean Beeby, "Liberals leave royal position vacant in Queen's Sapphire Jubilee year," *CBC News*, September 19, 2017, cbc.ca/news/politics/queen-canadian-secretary-royal-visits-heritage-1.4295322.
4. McCreery, "Confidant and Chief of Staff."
5. Ibid.
6. Ibid.
7. The Governor General of Canada, "Our Structure," accessed June 1, 2019, gg.ca/en/the-office/structure.
8. Government of Canada, "Rideau Cottage," accessed June 1, 2019, pc.gc.ca/apps/dfhd/page_fhbro_eng.aspx?id=2716.
9. McCreery, "Confidant and Chief of Staff."
10. Marie-Danielle Smith and Brian Platt, "Failure to launch: Inside Julie Payette's turbulent first year as Governor General," *National Post*, September 21, 2018, nationalpost.com/news/politics/failure-to-launch-inside-julie-payettes-turbulent-first-year-as-governor-general.

11. McCreery, "Confidant and Chief of Staff."
12. Beeby, "Liberals leave royal position vacant."
13. Kevin MacLeod, interview by Dale Smith, April 1, 2019.
14. Ibid.
15. Ibid.
16. Christopher McCreery, "Subtle Yet Significant Innovations: The Advisory Committee on Vice-Regal Appointments and the Secretary's New Royal Powers," in *La Couronne et le Parlement / The Crown and Parliament*, ed. Michel Bédard and Philippe Lagassé (Montreal: Éditions Yvon Blais, 2015).
17. Kevin MacLeod, interview.
18. Ibid.
19. Ibid.
20. Ibid.
21. Ibid.
22. Beeby, "Liberals leave royal position vacant."
23. Donald Booth, interview by Dale Smith, November 8, 2019.
24. Ibid.

PART THREE

MOVING TOWARD A NEW REIGN

THE SUCCESSION TO THE THRONE IN CANADA

Warren J. Newman

Introduction

The succession to the throne must always be, regardless of circumstances, a matter of some delicacy. The accession by one king or queen to the throne of his or her royal predecessor is a relatively rare and solemn event, not the least because it is normally occasioned by the decease of a reigning monarch.

In the case of our present sovereign, Her Majesty Elizabeth II, we have been blessed by the steady reign of a remarkably gracious Queen: "long may she reign," as the anthem commands. Gracious not only in her regal dignity and bearing, but in her dedication. One need only recall the public vow she

* Senior General Counsel, Constitutional, Administrative and International Law Section, Department of Justice of Canada. The views expressed in this chapter are those of the author in his academic capacity and do not bind the Department of Justice or the Government of Canada.

made to the peoples of the Commonwealth on her twenty-first birthday,[1] while still princess and heiress to the throne: "I declare before you that my whole life whether it be long or short shall be devoted to your service and the service of our great imperial family to which we all belong."

Since the decease of her father, King George VI, in February 1952, Queen Elizabeth II has become the longest-reigning British monarch, the first to celebrate a Sapphire Jubilee,[2] and the longest-serving head of state. And if her longevity is similar to that of the late Queen Mother,[3] then there may be good reason to expect that we shall be celebrating her Platinum Jubilee in 2022. Still, the reign of the Queen will draw to a peaceful end, one day, and thus it is that we must contemplate the matter of the succession to the throne, notably in Canada.

The Law and Custom Governing the Succession to the Throne

The succession to the throne must be distinguished in law from the formal coronation, which today is essentially religious and ceremonial in character.[4] Upon the demise of the Queen, Prince Charles will become King of the United Kingdom, Canada, and his other realms and territories immediately. There will be no interregnum. The accession to the throne of a new sovereign upon the death of the preceding one is recognized by the Accession Council and promulgated throughout the realms. The new King will thus be king well before he is crowned and anointed. So it was with Edward VIII, who acceded to the throne as King on January 20, 1936, immediately upon the death of his father, George V, but who abdicated that throne in the midst of a constitutional crisis (precipitated principally by his own actions) on December 11, 1936.

It was not always thus. As J.G. Noppen has written:

> In early times the prince elect was not King until he had been shown to the people, accepted as their sovereign lord, anointed, and crowned. Richard I is styled Duke of Normandy in the contemporary account of the procession

from the Hall to the Abbey church. The custom was not a good one, as the lawless elements were inclined to take advantage of the *interregnum*, and to obviate this the eldest son of the King was sometimes crowned during his father's lifetime. From the time of Edward I, however, the King's reign has been considered to begin from the moment of the predecessor's passing.[5]

The modern understanding is well-explained in Wade and Phillips, *Constitutional Law*:

> There are two ceremonies which mark the accession of the new Sovereign. Immediately on the death of his predecessor the Sovereign is proclaimed, not by the Privy Council as such, but by the Lords Spiritual and Temporal and other leading citizens, a body which is a survival of an old assemblage, which met to choose and proclaim the King. The Proclamation is afterwards approved at the first meeting of the new King's Privy Council. After an interval of time follows the Coronation, the ancient ceremony which gave religious sanction to title by election and brought to a close the interregnum, when no King reigned, between the death of one King and the election of his successor. Anson noted that, as the recognition of hereditary rights strengthened, the importance of the election and coronation dwindled, while the great practical inconvenience of the interregnum, the abeyance of the King's Peace, was curtailed.[6]

Reference may also be had to the following account of the accession to the throne in O. Hood Phillips and Jackson, *Constitutional and Administrative Law*:

> When a Sovereign dies his successor accedes to the Throne immediately. The automatic succession of the new monarch is sometimes expressed in the maxim "the King never

dies." At common law a person is never too young to succeed to the Throne.

As soon as conveniently possible after the death or abdication of a Sovereign, an Accession Council meets to acclaim the new Sovereign. An Accession Council is composed of the Lords Spiritual and Temporal, assisted by members of the Privy Council, with the Lord Mayor and Aldermen of the City of London and the high commissioners of the Commonwealth countries. The new Sovereign takes the oath for the security of the Presbyterian Church in Scotland prescribed by the Union with Scotland Act 1706. Before the first meeting of Parliament or at his coronation he must declare that he is a faithful Protestant, and promise to uphold the enactment securing the Protestant succession to the Throne.[7]

The common law relating to the succession to the throne was gradually supplemented, and in many important respects, supplanted and superseded, by acts of the Parliaments of England, Great Britain, and the United Kingdom.[8] The most significant of these in relation to modern times have been the English *Bill of Rights* of 1688, the *Act of Settlement* of 1700, and, more recently, the *Statute of Westminster, 1931*, the *Abdication Act* of 1936, and the *Succession to the Crown Act, 2013*.

The Canadian Context of Law, Principle, and Convention

In the Canadian context, the core principles of hereditary and constitutional monarchy under law have come to us through the preamble of the *British North America Act* — now styled the *Constitution Act, 1867* — which vouchsafes for Canada a "Dominion under the Crown of the United Kingdom," with "a Constitution similar in Principle to that of the United Kingdom." It should be emphasized in this regard that the substantive body of law relating to royal succession remains alterable, from time to time, by the Parliament of the United Kingdom. Our fundamental rule of recognition, in this regard, is simple and effective: it provides that whoever is the sovereign — the reigning king or queen — of the United Kingdom, as determined by the law of the United Kingdom, is perforce the King or Queen of Canada.[9]

This is not to suggest that the *Succession to the Crown Act, 2013* enacted by the Parliament of the United Kingdom extends to Canada, as Canada's own road to sovereignty as an independent state, beginning with the Balfour Report of 1926 and the *Statute of Westminster, 1931*, and culminating in the *Canada Act, 1982*, means that since 1982 "No Act of the Parliament of the United Kingdom passed after the *Constitution Act, 1982* comes into force shall extend to Canada as part of its law."[10]

Nor does it mean, however, that Canada can exert no influence over the evolution of the British law of royal succession. The preamble to the *Statute of Westminster, 1931* — itself an instrument that is part of the Constitution of Canada — sets out an important rule of constitutional convention as between the United Kingdom Parliament and the Dominion Parliaments, including the Parliament of Canada:

> And whereas *it is meet and proper to set out by way of preamble to this Act that*, inasmuch as *the Crown is the symbol of the free association of the members of the British Commonwealth* of Nations, and as they are *united by a common allegiance to the Crown, it would be in accord with the established constitutional position of all the members of the Commonwealth* in relation to one another *that any alteration to the law touching the Succession to the Throne* or the Royal Style and Titles *shall hereafter require the assent* as well *of the Parliaments of all of the Dominions* as of the Parliament of the United Kingdom. (emphasis added) [11]

So it was that the Parliament of Canada, by the *Succession to the Throne Act* of 1937, signified its assent to the alteration in the law touching the succession to the throne effected by the *His Majesty's Declaration of Abdication Act* enacted by the Parliament of the United Kingdom in December 1936;[12] and so, too, it was that the Parliament of Canada, by the *Succession to the Throne*

Act, 2013, assented to the alteration in the law produced by the *Succession to the Crown Act, 2013* enacted by the United Kingdom Parliament.

In fact, the Canadian statutory precedents maintaining respect for this constitutional convention include the changes that occurred to the royal style and titles in 1947 and 1953. The convention, as recited in the preamble, requires the assent "of the Parliaments of all the Dominions" for alterations not only to the law respecting the succession to the throne but also "the Royal Style and Titles." Thus, when King George VI proceeded to relinquish the title of "Emperor of India," the Parliament of Canada enacted the *Royal Style and Titles Act* of 1947. That act, after repeating, in its own preamble, the terms of the recital from the *Statute of Westminster* set out above, went on to assent to the alteration in the single operative provision of the act: "The assent of the Parliament of Canada is hereby given to the omission from the Royal Style and Titles the words 'Indiae Imperator' and the words 'Emperor of India.'"[13]

Our Queen acceded to the throne upon the decease of her father in 1952 and in December of that year, representatives of the Commonwealth countries assembled in London considered "the form of the Royal Style and Titles" and concluded that "it would be in accord with the established constitutional position that each member country should use for its own purposes a form suitable to its own particular circumstances but retaining a substantial element common to all." They agreed "to take such action as is necessary in each country to secure the appropriate constitutional approval" for the changes envisaged. Once again, the Parliament of Canada proceeded by way of simple assent, through the *Royal Style and Titles Act* of 1953, to the issuance, by Her Majesty, of a royal proclamation establishing for Canada the following royal style and titles:

> Elizabeth the Second, by the Grace of God of the United Kingdom, Canada and Her other Realms and Territories Queen, Head of the Commonwealth, Defender of the Faith.
>
> Elizabeth Deux, par la grâce de Dieu Reine du Royaume-Uni, du Canada et de ses autres royaumes et territoires, Chef du Commonwealth, Défenseur de la Foi.[14]

There are those who would dismiss the continuing relevance of these Canadian statutory precedents, or who would claim that the constitutional convention they vindicate has been abandoned by some of the other Commonwealth realms. Those views, however, misapprehend the significance of the role that constitutional conventions — and notably this convention — continue to play in the Canadian context and constitutional framework.

As the Supreme Court of Canada observed in the *Patriation Reference*, the importance of constitutional conventions lies in the constitutional principle or value they are designed to protect. Indeed, the Supreme Court recognized that some constitutional conventions are more important than certain legal provisions precisely because these conventional rules are the means by which a pivotal constitutional principle is preserved and maintained.[15]

The convention recorded in the second recital of the preamble to the *Statute of Westminster, 1931* has always been treated as pivotally important in Canada because it protects the principle of the equality and autonomy of the Commonwealth countries in relation to the United Kingdom and each other, while recognizing that those which have the Queen (and previously, the King) as head of state are freely "united by a common allegiance to the Crown." The rule expressed in that convention is that because of that equality and autonomy, but also that common allegiance, changes to the law of succession to the throne or the royal style and titles "shall require the assent ... of the Parliaments of all of the Dominions," as well as that of the Parliament of the United Kingdom.

The Parliament of Canada's assenting statutes — the *Succession to the Throne Act* of 1937, the *Royal Style and Titles Act* of 1947, the *Royal Style and Titles Act* of 1953, and the *Succession to the Throne Act* of 2013 — were all patently directed toward hallowing that convention and thus upholding the important constitutional principles behind it. Professor Vernon Bogdanor put it well in his book, *The Monarchy and the Constitution*:[16] the evolution toward a "locally variable title" was one thing, but "with regard to the succession, however, it was essential to retain a common rule so that the Commonwealth monarchies should not be a personal union over a fortuitous conglomeration of territories.... It remains, therefore, a convention that any alteration in these rules must be agreed between all the members of the Commonwealth which recognize the Queen as their head of state."

While "the unity of the *title* of the sovereign" might henceforth admit of some adaptation to local conditions, it would have been "constitutionally inappropriate" to deviate from "the unity of the *person* of the sovereign."[17]

The Canadian *Succession to the Throne Act, 2013*

The *Succession to the Throne Act, 2013* thus signified the Parliament of Canada's assent to an alteration in the law touching the succession to the throne that was contemplated in a bill that was then in the process of enactment by the United Kingdom Parliament, which, pursuant to the prior agreement of the representatives of those realms "of which Her Majesty is Sovereign," would abrogate the common-law rule of male primogeniture (thereby no longer making royal succession depend on gender) and end the legal disqualification arising from an heir to the throne marrying a Roman Catholic.

The Canadian statute was, as explained above, enacted in furtherance of the constitutional convention recited in the preamble to the *Statute of Westminster, 1931* (itself a part of the Constitution of Canada) requiring assent to such alterations to the law of royal succession or the royal style and titles not just by the United Kingdom Parliament but also by the Dominion parliaments, including Canada's. The Canadian approach was supported, in the view of the minister of justice and attorney general of Canada, not only by sound legal principle but also by Canadian practice and tradition, as manifested in the three precedents dealing with changes relating to the succession to the throne[18] or the royal style and titles, in which the Parliament of Canada had also signified its assent by statute.[19]

Moreover, the Canadian *Succession to the Throne Act, 2013* was particularly well-adapted to the Canadian context. It maintained Canada's control over changes to the law of royal succession by maintaining respect for the constitutional convention that had been followed in Canada and the United Kingdom since the enactment of the *Statute of Westminster, 1931* and the Parliament of Canada's first *Succession to the Throne Act* in 1937. It was also, within the gamut of legal options ostensibly available or perhaps mooted in academic circles as desirable, the one that was clearly within the realm of the possible. The Parliament of Canada, in its wisdom, chose that option.

A pragmatic approach to achieving the modernization of the legal rules of royal succession does not mean it was an unprincipled approach. The Parliament of Canada's assent to the changes to the rules proposed in 2013 by the United Kingdom's legislation was predicated upon Canadian legal and political constitutionalism, and respect for the principles of hereditary and constitutional monarchy, the rule of law, constitutional convention, parliamentary sovereignty, and democracy. It also advanced Canadian values with respect to ameliorating the equality of status among male and female heirs to the throne, as well as reducing religious discrimination. That approach was also based on legislative precedents and an understanding of the Canadian constitutional framework that acknowledges, as part of the basic institutional structure, a principle of symmetry that is embodied in a rule of automatic recognition or identification of the sovereign.

Simply put, the Queen of Canada is recognized as such because she is the Queen of the United Kingdom, as determined by the law of succession to the Crown of the United Kingdom, which body of law may be amended from time to time by the Parliament of the United Kingdom. That rule of automatic recognition of the Queen — or, at some future date, the new King — as the Sovereign is a basic imperative of Canadian constitutional law, and it is inherent to the structure of our Constitution and its monarchical and parliamentary institutions and tradition. A change to that fundamental rule of symmetry and Sovereign identification might well require a constitutional amendment in Canada, if Canadians were to decide one day to adopt a different rule. Not so a statute like the *Succession to the Throne Act, 2013*, which respects the actual constitutional structure and implements the constitutional convention of parliamentary assent to alterations to the law of royal succession that is expressly contemplated in the preamble to the *Statute of Westminster, 1931*.

The objections to the Canadian approach, as voiced by academics such as Anne Twomey and Philippe Lagassé,[20] ranged from the viewpoint that changing the rules of royal succession would require the Commonwealth parliaments to amend directly the text of the venerable British statutes, the *Bill of Rights* and *Act of Settlement*, insofar as they could be held to apply to the realm countries; to requiring, at least in Canada, the arduous and uncertain pursuit of a constitutional amendment under the unanimous consent procedure of section 41 of the *Constitution Act, 1982*, on the theory that the changes contemplated were nothing short of a constitutional alteration to the office of the Queen. Indeed, the parliaments of Australia and New Zealand did enact legislation mirroring the United Kingdom's *Succession to the Crown Act, 2013*, which amended the text of the *Bill of Rights* and the *Act of Settlement* and repealed the *Royal Marriages Act* of 1772 (although neither the governments nor the parliaments of Australia and New Zealand advanced the position that the statutes were themselves constitutional amendments).

From the standpoint of the Canadian government and other academics and constitutional lawyers,[21] these objections amounted to a misapprehension of the legal and constitutional position that obtained in Canada, and also demonstrated the pitfalls inherent in treating the constitutional frameworks of the realms as if they were identical and required identical approaches to the question of the succession to the throne. The pre-eminent constitutional scholar and lawyer Peter W. Hogg has written:

> My conclusion is that the changes to the rules of succession that are enacted by the U.K.'s *Succession to the Crown Act 2013* have had the automatic effect of changing the rules of succession for Canada too. That is not because a U.K. law can apply in Canada — it cannot, not even with the consent of Canada. It is because the Constitution of Canada implicitly provides that the Queen of Canada is the same person as the Queen of the United Kingdom and the other Commonwealth Realms. All that Canada needs to do to preserve that constitutional principle of symmetry is to follow the convention declared in the *Statute of Westminster* and enact an Act of Parliament providing the Parliament of Canada's "assent" to the U.K. Bill. That has now been accomplished by the *Succession to the Throne Act, 2013*. No change in Canadian law is required, and, in particular, no amendment of the Constitution of Canada is required.[22]

Far from "de-Canadianizing" the Crown, "de-patriating" the Canadian constitution, or retreating from the implications of Canada's independence as a sovereign state, as some of its detractors have claimed, the *Succession to the Throne Act, 2013* is a clear expression of that independence: the signifying of the solemn assent of a sovereign Canadian Parliament to changes agreed to and concurred in by the members of a "free association" of states united by "a common allegiance to the Crown."

Professor (and now Dean of Law at Queen's University) Mark Walters, in his cogent essay, "Succession to the Throne and the Architecture of the Constitution of Canada," identifies "two basic ways by which a realm may recognize the King or Queen of the United Kingdom as its King or Queen." The first is by what he calls a rule of Crown identification (and others, as mentioned above, have called a rule of symmetry or recognition) whereby, as in Canada, the King or Queen is "that person who, at the relevant time, is the person who is the King or Queen of the United Kingdom under the laws of royal succession in force there." This "simple rule of Crown identification" thus renders the enactment of a domestic, substantive law of royal succession "unnecessary." The second way is where a realm (such as Australia) chooses to have its own law of royal succession by incorporating, as the substance of that domestic law, "the same body of law that governs royal succession in the United Kingdom." (Professor Walters terms this an "incorporated law of royal succession."[23]) He adds:

> Is a realm with a rule of Crown identification less independent or sovereign than a realm with an incorporated law of Crown succession? No. At any time, the realm with a rule of Crown identification can amend its law to adopt a different rule for identifying its monarch, or to abolish its monarchy altogether. Until then, the effect of the rule is simply to spare the realm the burden of having to amend its own law each time the law of royal succession in the United Kingdom changes....
>
> Once the commitment is made by a state to recognize the Crown in the United Kingdom as its Crown, the rule of Crown identification seems much simpler and more

efficient than having an incorporated law of Crown succession. However, the legacy of the British empire casts a long shadow. For a realm that still feels insecure about its image as an independent state, the symbolic value of changing its own law each time the law of royal succession is changed in the United Kingdom may be important politically. Even so, it should be understood that this symbolism comes at a very high price in terms of constitutional architecture. By adopting an incorporated law of Crown succession, the realm will have to accept into its own constitutional law large swathes of law that really only make sense in light of the social and religious history of England.... There are sound reasons for why an independent and sovereign state may prefer having a rule of Crown identification over an incorporated law of Crown succession.[24]

Political scientist Andrew Heard, a well-known expert in the role of constitutional conventions in Canada, makes a similar point:

Canada shares a link with the 15 other realms which honours a common bond while celebrating the independence and diversity of the Queen's realms.... Canada finds good company in most of the overseas realms which are proudly independent nations and yet accept that the Queen of the United Kingdom acts as their sovereign. There is little need for Canada to go beyond a political and cultural localization that embraces the monarch without appropriating her.[25]

Fellow political scientist Philippe Lagassé, although still disputing the pedigree of the *Succession to the Throne Act, 2013* — in his opinion, Canadian governments held "opposite views" on "how to alter the laws of royal succession for Canada in 1936 and 2013," and "constitutional politics," rather than the demands of constitutional law, motivated those views — has offered a clear-eyed, unsentimental assessment:

While Canada is no longer a loyal Dominion of the British Empire, patriation has revived the notion that Canada is ultimately under the Crown of the United Kingdom in matters related to the monarchy. In the end, this arrangement may survive any further change since it provides a workable, typically Canadian, compromise: an independent Canadian state headed by a British monarchy that helps to avoid constitutional tensions.[26]

A challenge to the validity of the *Succession to the Throne Act, 2013* was roundly rejected by the Superior Court of Quebec in February 2016.[27] An appeal of that judgment was heard by the Quebec Court of Appeal in February 2018.

On October 28, 2019, the Court of Appeal issued a unanimous decision dismissing the appeal. The Court of Appeal held that the principle of symmetry between the Queen of the United Kingdom and the Queen of Canada is well anchored ("bien ancré") in the Constitution of Canada, notably through the preamble and the key provisions of the *Constitution Act, 1867*, and that constitutional experts such as professors Walters, Pelletier, and Hogg agree that the principle of symmetry, flowing from a harmonious political desire to share the same monarch, is part of our Canadian constitutional law. As well, this rule or principle of symmetry is consistent with other principles, including federalism and the rule of law. The provisions of British statutes such as the English *Bill of Rights* and the *Act of Settlement* are not themselves entrenched as part of the Constitution of Canada; what Canada has inherited, through "a Constitution similar in Principle to that of the United Kingdom," are the broader principles (such as a constitutional monarchy, hereditary royal succession, parliamentary sovereignty, and judicial independence) that underlie such provisions. Nor did the Parliament of Canada, in enacting the *Succession to the Throne Act* of 1937, intend to incorporate by reference the British rules of royal succession such as to entrench them as part of Canadian constitutional law. Nor, the Court of Appeal ruled, did the changes made to the rules of royal succession by the United Kingdom Parliament in 2013 have any effect ("*n'ont aucune incidence*") on the office of the Queen in Canada. The Canadian

Succession to the Throne Act, 2013 did not change the powers, the status, or the constitutional role of the Queen and thus was not aimed at the "office of the Queen," as protected by the unanimous consent procedure for amendments under paragraph 41 (*a*) of the *Constitution Act, 1982*.

The Court of Appeal thus agreed with the trial court that the *Succession to the Throne Act, 2013* was consistent with Canada's constitutional framework and principles and with statutory precedents that gave effect to a convention recorded in the preamble to the *Statute of Westminster, 1931*, to the effect that Dominion Parliaments as well as the United Kingdom Parliament ought to consent to alterations to the law touching the succession to the throne and the royal style and titles. The Court of Appeal, like the trial court, also rejected other arguments based on constitutional requirements relating to bilingual enactment of legislation (which were respected by Parliament) and on freedom of religion (which was not affected in Canada).[28]

Accession to the Throne in 1952

In contemplating not simply the niceties of the law but also the solemn events leading to the succession to the throne, it is wise to begin with what transpired when our reigning monarch acceded to the throne in 1952. King George VI died peacefully in his sleep in the early hours of February 6 of that year. Immediately, Princess Elizabeth became the new sovereign. She was, in fact, some 4,500 miles away in Kenya when her husband, Prince Philip, told her the tragic news. The subsequent flight to London took close to twenty hours. Among the first to greet her upon landing on February 7 were Winston Churchill, the prime minister, and Clement Attlee, the leader of the opposition. The new Queen was then driven to Clarence House, where she was welcomed by her grandmother, Queen Mary, and then spoke on the telephone to her mother, now the Queen Mother, at Sandringham.

The Accession Council met twice: first at 5:00 p.m. on February 6 to make its proclamation declaring the accession of the new sovereign, and then, in the Queen's presence, on February 8. The Accession Council was composed of privy councillors, officers of state, the Lord Mayor of London, the Court of Aldermen, and the high commissioners of the realms. The Accession Council was presided over by the Lord President of the Council. The clerk of the council read the proclamation, as follows:

> Whereas it has pleased Almighty God to call to His Mercy our late Sovereign Lord King George the Sixth of Blessed and Glorious memory, by whose Decease the Crown is solely and rightfully come to the High and Mighty Princess Elizabeth Alexandra Mary: We, therefore, the Lords Spiritual and Temporal of this Realm, being here assisted with these His late Majesty's Privy Council, with representatives of other Members of the Commonwealth, with other Principal Gentlemen of Quality, with the Lord Mayor, Aldermen, and Citizens of London, do now hereby with one voice and Consent of Tongue and Heart publish and proclaim that the High and Mighty Princess Elizabeth Alexandra Mary is now, by the death of our late Sovereign of happy memory, become Queen Elizabeth the Second, by the Grace of God Queen of this Realm and of all Her other Realms and Territories, Head of the Commonwealth, Defender of the Faith, to whom Her lieges do acknowledge all Faith and constant Obedience with hearty and humble Affection, beseeching God by whom Kings and Queens do reign, to bless the Royal Princess Elizabeth the Second with long and happy Years to reign over us.[29]

At 10:00 a.m. on February 8, at what was effectively her first Privy Council meeting, Her Majesty made the following declaration, her words carrying the emotion and the weight of that solemn and sombre occasion:

> By the sudden death of my dear Father, I am called to assume the duties and responsibilities of Sovereignty. At this time of deep sorrow, it is a profound consolation to me to be assured of the sympathy which you and all my

Peoples feel towards me … My heart is too full for me to say more to you today than that I shall always work, as my Father did throughout his Reign, to uphold constitutional government and to advance the happiness and prosperity of my Peoples, spread as they are all the world over. I know that in my resolve to follow his shining example of service and devotion, I shall be inspired by the loyalty and affection of those whose Queen I have been called to be, and by the Counsel of their elected Parliaments. I pray that God will help me to discharge worthily this heavy task that has been laid upon me so early in my life.[30]

After making her declaration, the new Queen took the oath prescribed by the *Act of Union* of 1707 to maintain the Protestant religion and the Presbyterian Church of Scotland.

At 11:00 a.m., the proclamation of the accession of Her Majesty Queen Elizabeth II was read from the balcony of St. James's Palace by Garter King of Arms, Sir George Bellow, in the presence of the officers of the College of Heralds, including the hereditary Earl Marshal, the Duke of Norfolk. The proclamation would be repeated elsewhere in London and in the principal cities of England, Scotland, and Wales, and throughout the Commonwealth.

Canada was, in fact, the first of the new Queen's realms to issue its own proclamation. Prime Minister Louis St. Laurent had been awakened at 6:00 a.m. on February 6 with the news of the King's death. The Canadian Press reported that official word of the King's decease had come to Canada in a cablegram to Chief Justice Thibaudeau Rinfret, acting as administrator of the Government of Canada, from the King's private secretary. The cable read: "Profoundly regret to state that His Majesty King George the Sixth passed away peacefully in his sleep early this morning." The Canadian Cabinet was convened, and dealt with two proclamations: the first proclaiming Elizabeth as Queen and the second directing government officials who held commissions from the late King to continue in office.

The proclamation of accession was read to twenty-three members of the Queen's Privy Council for Canada. It declared as follows:

WHEREAS it hath pleased Almighty God to call to His Mercy our late Sovereign Lord King George the Sixth of blessed and glorious memory by whose decease the Crown of Great Britain, Ireland and all other His late Majesty's dominions is solely and rightfully come to the High and Mighty Princess Elizabeth Alexandra Mary, Now Know Ye that I, the said Right Honourable Thibeaudeau Rinfret, Administrator of Canada as aforesaid, assisted by Her Majesty's Privy Council for Canada do now hereby with one voice and consent of tongue and heart, publish and proclaim that the High and Mighty Princess Elizabeth Alexandra Mary is now by the death of Our late Sovereign of happy and glorious memory become our only lawful and rightful Liege Lady Elizabeth the Second by the Grace of God, of Great Britain, Ireland and the British Dominions beyond the Seas Queen, Defender of the Faith, Supreme Liege Lady in and over Canada, to whom we acknowledge all faith and constant obedience with all hearty and humble affection, beseeching God by whom all Kings and Queens do reign to bless the Royal Princess Elizabeth the Second with long and happy years to reign over us.[31]

The Accession Declaration of Elizabeth II was made on November 4, 1952, prior to the Queen's first speech to Parliament. It read: "I, ELIZABETH do solemnly and sincerely in the presence of God profess, testify, and declare that I am a faithful Protestant, and that I will, according to the true intent of the enactments which secure the Protestant succession to the Throne, uphold and maintain the said enactments to the best of my powers according to law."

The Coronation in 1953

As we have noted above, the Coronation ceremony is imbued with spiritual meaning and religious tradition as well as ritual symbolism and pageantry, but it is not, as it was in ancient times, synonymous with accession. The Coronation occurs several months or more after the accession of the sovereign. Edward VIII was King but never crowned and anointed before his abdication. The subsequent coronations of George VI in 1937, and certainly that of Elizabeth II in 1953, are still within the living memory of many Canadians.

The major steps in the Coronation service include the Recognition (the popular acceptance of the Queen as sovereign); the taking of the Oath (to govern by and to maintain the laws of her peoples); the Anointing (by which the Queen was consecrated); the Investiture with the Sword of State, the Robe Royal, the delivery of the Orb and Sceptre, the Rod of Equity and Mercy, and other regalia, all symbols of her royal office; as well as the Crowning (with St. Edward's Crown), the Benediction, and the Enthroning.

In taking the oath at the Coronation at Westminster Abbey on June 2, 1953, Her Majesty solemnly promised and swore to govern the peoples of the United Kingdom, Canada, Australia, New Zealand, and her other possessions and territories "according to their respective laws and customs," and to cause "Law and Justice, in Mercy" to be executed in all her judgments. That promise reminds us that while the Queen's realms may, up to a point, have similar constitutional institutions and arrangements, the laws, customs, and conventions of countries such as Canada, Australia, and New Zealand are not identical and may require distinct approaches to achieving common ends.

The Next Succession to the Throne

The next succession to the throne will in all likelihood, at least in material respects, preserve the sense of solemn occasion, tradition, continuity, and ceremony evident in previous royal successions. As already emphasized, as a matter of law, there will be no interregnum and Prince Charles will accede to the throne immediately. The Accession Council will meet and proclaim him King (either as Charles III or perhaps under the regnal name of George VII). The Coronation ceremony will take place at an appropriate moment, some months later. The protocol recording the essential or customary steps in the proceedings of the Accession Council in relation to the proclamation of the new sovereign has been set out by the Privy Council Office and is available for public consultation online.[32] These steps do not differ in material respects from those undertaken in respect of the accession of Queen Elizabeth II in 1952. Once again, the Accession Council will meet in two parts: first, to take actions as the Privy Council (and without the sovereign) to proclaim the new sovereign and to make certain orders of Council that are consequential upon the proclamation; and second, by way of the holding by the sovereign of his or her first Privy Council meeting. The Commonwealth high commissioners (including the fifteen who represent the sovereign's realms beyond the United Kingdom) would likely be received after the Privy Council proceedings.

In Canada, by virtue of the preamble and section 9 of the *Constitution Act, 1867*, the executive government and authority "of and over Canada" will be vested in the new King from the moment Charles accedes to the throne. The King's Privy Council for Canada will meet and the governor general or the chief administrator will read the proclamation of accession. As for the Parliament of Canada, section 2 of the *Parliament of Canada Act* provides: "Parliament shall not determine or be dissolved by the demise of the Crown and, notwithstanding the demise, shall continue, and may meet, convene and sit, in the same manner as if that demise had not happened."

Robert Hazell and Bob Morris have done some remarkable forward thinking on behalf of the Constitution Unit at University College London on whether it is appropriate to modernize or reformulate aspects of the accession declaration and the statutory coronation oaths, to produce texts perhaps more in keeping with these ecumenical and even secular times. They have, to this end, drafted a series of proposals, ranging from "radical reformulation" to more modest and incremental change. "If there is not the political will to legislate," they write, "the government should consider preparing a statement to give to Parliament on accession explaining the historical reasons for the oaths, and how they are to be understood in modern times."[33]

If the Parliament of the United Kingdom were indeed to proceed to alter the oaths by statutory amendments, whether such alterations would be subject, as a matter of constitutional convention, to the rule expressed in the second recital of the preamble to the *Statute of Westminster, 1931* and thus require the assent of the parliaments of the other realms (including that of Canada) is an interesting question. The authors of the paper recognize the importance of the Commonwealth realms and that their position "has to be borne in mind whenever changes to the U.K. crown's status are being considered, as in the case of the Succession to the Throne Act 2013." However, "their consent is only required where there are proposals — which this paper does not canvass — to change the rules of royal succession or the royal style and titles, but their interests should not be ignored."[34]

While changes to the oaths *consequent upon* statutory alterations to the law touching the succession to the throne (such as repealing the legislative provisions regulating the maintenance of the Protestant line of succession) would probably be contemplated by the convention, changes that simply relax or soften some of the language in the oaths, without fundamentally altering the current legal rules of royal succession themselves, may not be caught by the convention. That said, as the authors of the paper acknowledged, it would be prudent to consult the interests of the Commonwealth realms, even where legislative action by Commonwealth parliaments may not be necessary, even from a conventional point of view.

It may be noted here, as well, that if the royal style and titles relating to the new sovereign are not altered in material respects from those proclaimed in 1953, there may be no need for an additional Canadian statute at the time of the accession or coronation. It should be recalled that the *Royal Style and Titles Acts* enacted by the Parliament of Canada in 1947 and 1953 were required by constitutional convention precisely because the style and titles were being altered: in 1947 by the removal of the title of "Emperor of India"; in 1953 by the addition of a particularized element (the mention of "Canada") and the addition of the title "Head of the Commonwealth." Unless additional material changes are contemplated, further legislative action by the Parliament of Canada may not be required, unless, of course, it is thought politic that the Canadian Parliament should be seen to authorize the proclamation of the style and titles pertaining to the new sovereign, Charles, whether or not the style and titles have been substantially altered.[35]

Conclusion

The *Constitution Act, 1867* vouchsafed for Canada the federal union of the original provinces in "One Dominion under the Crown of the United

Kingdom," with "a Constitution similar in Principle to that of the United Kingdom." Canada is now an independent state, but it remains a constitutional monarchy with "a common allegiance to the Crown" as recognized by the *Statute of Westminster, 1931*, itself a part of the Constitution of Canada. Whoever is the Queen or King of the United Kingdom, as determined by the law of succession of the United Kingdom, is perforce the Queen or King of Canada. This fundamental rule of automatic recognition (or Crown symmetry or identification) does not deny the existence of a distinct Crown in right of Canada. What it does do is relieve Canada of the necessity of enacting separate, substantive rules of succession to that Crown that, if they are to ensure the succession of the same sovereign as that of the United Kingdom, would need to mirror the laws of the United Kingdom each time they are amended.

If Canadians wish to alter the fundamental rule of automatic recognition, it lies within their power, acting through their political representatives, to authorize amendments to the Constitution of Canada to achieve that end. In the meantime, the force of a long-standing constitutional convention embodied in the preamble to the *Statute of Westminster* ensures that the Parliament of Canada must assent to alterations in the law touching the succession to the throne, or the royal style and titles, enacted by the Parliament of the United Kingdom, which in turn ensures that consultations will take place between the government of the United Kingdom and the government of Canada (and those of the other realms) before such changes are put forward and implemented. This rule of constitutional convention is a pivotal one because it protects the constitutional principles of the autonomy and the equality of those members of the Commonwealth that still share a cosmopolitan monarchy that originates in the United Kingdom.

The succession to the throne in Canada is thus foreordained by law and convention. The accession of Charles as the next King will be occasioned by the sadness and solemnity accompanying the loss, to this world, of a great and noble Queen. There will, however, be a legal certainty in the succession, and legal certainty and stability at a time of epochal change are a tribute to the resiliency of our constitutional monarchy under the rule of law.

Notes

1. On April 21, 1947.
2. On February 6, 1997 (marking sixty-five years of her reign).
3. Queen Elizabeth the Queen Mother lived until 101 years old.
4. See *Calvin's Case*, [1608] 7 Coke Reports 10b, 77 ER 377 at p. 389: "But the title is by descent; by Queen Elizabeth's death the Crown and kingdom of England descended to His Majesty, and he was fully and absolutely thereby King, without any essential, ceremony or act to be done ex post facto: for coronation is but a Royal ornament and solemnization of descent, but in no part of the title."
5. J.G. Noppen, *Royal Westminster and the Coronation* (London: Country Life, 1937), 79–80.
6. E.C.S. Wade and G. Godfrey Phillips, *Constitutional Law*, 4th ed. (London: Longmans, Green, 1950), 124–25. It has been said that an interregnum followed the decease of Edward VI in 1553; this was suspended when Lady Jane Grey was proclaimed Queen on July 10; nine days later, the Privy Council changed its view and proclaimed Mary as Queen instead, leading ultimately to Jane's condemnation on a charge of treason.
7. Paul Jackson and Patricia Leopold, *O. Hood Phillips and Jackson: Constitutional and Administrative Law*, 8th ed. (London: Sweet & Maxwell, 2001), at 14-003, 293–94. See the *Accession Declaration Act*, 1910 (U.K.), that replaced the earlier declaration that had been employed since 1689 and had used stronger terms against Catholic doctrine.
8. Consider, for example, during and in the aftermath of the tumultuous reign of Henry VIII, the first, second, and third *Succession to the Crown Acts* of 1533/34, 1536, and 1543/44; and the offence of high treason associated with interrupting the succession to the throne, or attempting to deprive the King or his successors of title, offences established by the *Treason Act* of 1547 (repealed by the *Treason Act, 1553*, but reinstated in part by the *Treason Act, 1554*).
9. This rule is inherent in the very structure of the Constitution of Canada, and is reflected in the preamble, in section 2 (repealed for

other reasons), in section 9, and in the oath of allegiance required under section 128 and set out in the fifth schedule to the *Constitution Act, 1867*.

10. *Canada Act, 1982*, section 2.

11. *Statute of Westminster, 1931*, preamble, second recital. "Dominion" was defined by section 1 of that act as meaning any of the following Dominions: "the Dominion of Canada, the Commonwealth of Australia, the Dominion of New Zealand, the Union of South Africa, the Irish Free State and Newfoundland." The schedule to the *Constitution Act, 1982*, read with subsection 52(2) of the latter act, makes the *Statute of Westminster, 1931* (as amended) part of the Constitution of Canada.

12. *His Majesty's Declaration of Abdication Act, 1936* was, in the view of the law officers of the Department of Justice, "*effective to vacate* former King Edward the Eighth's tenure of the Throne, *and to vest* the Succession to the Throne of the United Kingdom in the Heir Presumptive, the Duke of York." It followed that "the Duke of York having legally succeeded to the Throne of the United Kingdom as King George VI, the Executive Government and authority of and over Canada thereupon became," by virtue of the provisions of the *Constitution Act, 1867*, vested in the latter. "*This*, I apprehend, *was the legal position* whether the Government of Canada requested and consented [as in fact it did] to the enactment of His Majesty's Declaration of Abdication Act, 1936, *or not.*" (Emphasis added.) With respect to the second recital in the preamble to the *Statute of Westminster, 1931*, "This recital is not followed by any corresponding enactment. It is consequently no more than what its framers intended it to be, a statutory recognition of a constitutional convention." Charles Percy Plaxton, Memorandum for the Deputy Minister of Justice, January 11, 1937, pp. 3 and 9, Ernest Lapointe Fonds, archival ref. no. MG 27 III B 10 vol. 49, National Archives of Canada, Ottawa.

13. *Royal Style and Titles (Canada) Act, 1947*, 11 Geo. VI, c. 72, s. 2.

14. The proclamation, which was made on May 28, 1953, was published in Part I of the *Canada Gazette* of June 6, 1953, at 1674 (in English) and 1689 (in French).

15. *Reference re Resolution to amend the Constitution*, [1981] 1 S.C.R. 753, at 880: "The main purpose of constitutional conventions is to ensure that the legal framework of the constitution will be operated in accordance with the prevailing constitutional values or principles of the period. For example ... the constitutional value or principle which anchors the conventions regulating the relationship between the members of the Commonwealth is the independence of the former British colonies." And page 883: "It should be borne in mind that while they are not laws, some conventions may be more important than some laws. Their importance depends on the value or principle which they are meant to safeguard."

16. Vernon Bogdanor, *The Monarchy and the Constitution* (Oxford: Oxford University Press, 1995).

17. Ibid., 269.

18. The *Succession to the Throne Act*, S.C. 1937, c. 16, s. 1, signified the Parliament of Canada's assent, in accordance with the convention in the second recital of the preamble to the *Statute of Westminster, 1931*, to the "alteration in the law touching the Succession to the Throne" that had been enacted by *His Majesty's Declaration of Abdication Act, 1936*, a statute of the Parliament of the United Kingdom that gave legal effect to the Instrument of Abdication signed by King Edward VIII.

19. See the evidence of the Hon. Robert Nicholson, minister of justice and attorney general of Canada, in the Proceedings of the Standing Senate Committee on Legal and Constitutional Affairs on Bill C-53, An Act to Assent to Alterations in the Law Touching the Succession to the Throne, March 21, 2013; the minister's and government's position is also set out in "Changing the Line of Succession to the Throne," *Canadian Parliamentary Review* 36, no. 8 (2013). (I disclose that I appeared with the minister before the Senate Committee as the expert witness on behalf of the Department of Justice of Canada.)

20. Those critical of the Canadian approach have included professors Patrick Taillon and Geneviève Motard, who appeared as plaintiffs in an unsuccessful challenge to the validity of the statute, seconded by professor Anne Twomey, an expert in Australian constitutional law; Julien Fournier, a doctoral student; and André Binette, who, with Quebec practitioner André Jolicoeur, acted as their counsel.

Their views are expressed at length in Michel Bédard and Philippe Lagassé, eds., *La Couronne et le Parlement / The Crown and Parliament* (Montreal: Éditions Yvon Blais / Thomson-Reuters, 2015). See also Philippe Lagassé and Patrick Baud, "The Crown and Constitutional Amendment in Canada," in Bédard and Lagassé; Anne Twomey, "Royal Succession, Abdication, Regency and the Realms," *Review of Constitutional Studies* 22, no. 1 (2017): 33; and Garry Toffoli and Paul Benoit, "More is Needed to Change the Rules of Succession for Canada," *Canadian Parliamentary Review* 36, no. 10.

21. Including, in the study of the bill by the Senate Committee, evidence or submissions by professors Benoît Pelletier, Andrew Heard, and Mark Walters, as well (in the ensuing litigation in the *Motard* case) as an expert report presented on behalf of the Attorney General of Canada by professor Peter C. Oliver and entitled, "The Commonwealth, Constitutional Independence and Succession to the Throne"; see also Peter W. Hogg, "Succession to the Throne," *National Journal of Constitutional Law* 33 (2014): 83; Robert E. Hawkins, "'The Monarch is Dead: Long Live the Monarch': Canada's Assent to amending the Rules of Succession," *Journal of Parliamentary and Political Law* 7 (2013): 592; Mark D. Walters, "Succession to the Throne and the Architecture of the Constitution of Canada," in *La Couronne et le Parlement / The Crown and Parliament*, ed. Michel Bédard and Philippe Lagassé; Warren J. Newman, "Some Observations on the Queen, the Crown, the Constitution, and the Courts," *Review of Constitutional Studies* 22 (2017): 55; and Andrew Heard, "The Crown in Canada: Is There a Canadian Monarchy?" in *The Canadian Kingdom: 150 Years of Constitutional Monarchy*, ed. D. Michael Jackson (Toronto: Dundurn, 2018).

22. Peter W. Hogg, "Succession to the Throne," *National Journal of Constitutional Law* 33 (2014): 83–94.

23. Mark D. Walters, "Succession to the Throne and the Architecture of the Constitution of Canada," in *La Couronne et le Parlement / The Crown and Parliament*, ed. Michel Bédard and Philippe Lagassé.

24. Ibid., 269.

25. Andrew Heard, "The Crown in Canada: Is There a Canadian Monarchy?" in *The Canadian Kingdom: 150 Years of Constitutional Monarchy*, ed. D. Michael Jackson (Toronto: Dundurn, 2018).

26. Philippe Lagassé, "Royal Succession and the Constitutional Politics of the Canadian Crown, 1936–2013," *The Round Table* 107 (2018): 1 and 10.

27. *Motard and Taillon v. Canada (Attorney General)*, Superior Court of Quebec, No. 200-17-018455-130, February 18, 2016, *per* Bouchard J.S.C., official English translation of the reasons for judgment in French issued by the Court. (I disclose that I was one of counsel representing the Attorney General of Canada, both at trial and on the appeal.)

28. *Motard c. Canada*, Court of Appeal of Quebec, October 28, 2019, No 200-09-009233-161; *coram*: Kasirer, Gagnon, and Rancourt, J.J.; reasons for judgment by Jocelyn F. Rancourt, J.C.A.

29. Published in the *London Gazette*, February 8, 1952.

30. Reproduced in the *London Gazette*, February 12, 1952.

31. Published in the *Canada Gazette*, February 1952.

32. The Privy Council Office (U.K.), "The Accession Council," privycouncil.independent.gov.uk/privy-council/the-accession-council/.

33. Robert Hazell and Bob Morris, *Swearing in the New King: The Accession Declaration and Coronation Oaths*, (London: Constitution Unit, University College London, 2018), v. An excellent companion paper by Morris is entitled *Inaugurating a New Reign: Planning for Accession and Coronation* (London: Constitution Unit, University College London, 2018), ucl.ac.uk/constitution-unit/sites/constitution-unit/files/181_-_Inaugurating_a_New_Reign.pdf.

34. Ibid., *Swearing In the New King*, 2–3.

35. It is noteworthy that the *Oaths of Allegiance Act*, R.S.C. c. 0-1 provides, in section 2(2), that "where there is a demise of the Crown, there shall be substituted in the oath of allegiance the name of the Sovereign for the time being"; i.e., the regnal name of the new sovereign in the stead of Queen Elizabeth II. On the import of oaths of allegiance (particularly those of the *Citizenship Act* and the *Constitution Act, 1867*), see Serge Joyal, "The Oath of Allegiance: A New Perspective," in *The Canadian Kingdom*, ed. D. Michael Jackson.

CROWNING GLORY:
MONARCHY'S LITTLE-UNDERSTOOD CONTRIBUTION TO CANADA'S GREATNESS*

Brian Lee Crowley

Those of you who enjoy these things may have noticed a short satirical piece a few years ago in the *New Yorker*. Under the title "Queen Offers to Restore British Rule over United States," the author goes on to attribute to the Queen a fictitious speech in which she announces that, with America having made a hash of self-government, she is mercifully offering to bring the republic back under British rule.

Hilarious, right? Especially in the era of Donald Trump, who inevitably comes to mind when one reads "the Queen" opining on how America's great democratic experiment "did not end well." But might there be a serious point lurking beneath the veneer of satire?

In deciding whether to take up the Queen's offer to restore the status quo antebellum, Americans could do a lot worse than to inquire how that

* This essay is based on remarks delivered at the Monarchist League of Canada (Ottawa branch) on February 22, 2018.

other New World democracy, Canada, has fared as a parliamentary monarchy, and indeed how monarchy itself has evolved since the days of George III. Americans, and a lot of Canadians, might well be astonished to learn how very different our foundational assumptions are regarding the trappings and symbolism of power and national cohesion and unity, and how one might be able to argue that Canada comes out well from the comparison, due in no small part to our continued embrace of monarchy and the institution of the Crown.

To understand the real differences between monarchy and republicanism, it is less necessary to know about constitutions and prerogatives and thrones and legislatures than it is to understand what distinguishes two different casts of mind. Moreover, it is my belief that the dialogue of the deaf that often occurs between monarchists and republicans can be traced chiefly to these different casts of mind, and in particular to the value they attach to experience, to tradition, and to rationalism. No one, in my opinion, has better drawn the distinction between these two types of mind than Michael Oakeshott (and if you are not familiar with Oakeshott, I commend him to you). Listen to Oakeshott's description of the rationalist mind and see if it evokes for you a certain type of political thinker. He says:

> At bottom the Rationalist stands (he always *stands* for something) for independence of mind on all occasions, for thought free from obligation to any authority save the authority of 'reason' … He is the *enemy* of authority, of prejudice, of the merely traditional, customary or habitual. His mental attitude is at once sceptical and optimistic: sceptical because there is no opinion, no habit, no belief, nothing so firmly rooted or so widely held that he hesitates to question it and to judge it by what he calls his 'reason'; optimistic, because the rationalist never doubts the power of his 'reason,' when properly applied, to determine the worth of a thing, the truth of an opinion or the propriety of an action.… He is something also of an individualist, finding it difficult to believe that anyone who can think honestly and clearly will think differently from himself.

Of the alternative, traditionalist, or small-c conservative cast of mind, by contrast, Oakeshott has this to say:

> To be conservative is to prefer the familiar to the unfamiliar, to prefer the tried to the untried, fact to mystery, the actual to the possible, the limited to the unbounded, the near to the distant, the sufficient to the superabundant, the convenient to the perfect, present laughter to utopian bliss. Familiar relationships and loyalties will be preferred to the allure of more profitable attachments; to acquire and to enlarge will be less important than to keep, to cultivate and to enjoy; the grief of loss will be more acute than the excitement of novelty or promise.
>
> … the inclination to enjoy what is present and available is the opposite of ignorance and apathy and it breeds attachment and affection. Consequently, it is averse from change, which appears always, in the first place, as deprivation. A storm which sweeps away a copse and transforms a favourite view, the death of friends, the sleep of friendship, the desuetude of customs of behaviour, the retirement of a favourite clown, involuntary exile, reversals of fortune, the loss of abilities enjoyed and their replacement by others — these are changes, none perhaps without its compensations, which the man of conservative temperament unavoidably regrets.

Whatever can this have to do with a discussion of the merits of monarchy vs. republicanism? Why, everything, of course. Each of these casts of mind will, in the modern world, have a different answer to the question of "how ought people be ruled in a democracy?"

In understanding the different answers, it is important for me to clarify that Oakeshott is *not* saying that the traditionalist is an irrationalist, that he does not believe in the power of the human mind to understand and to solve humanity's problems. On the contrary, he is saying that when we engage in the project of "inventing" institutions from "first principles"; when individuals, committees, constitutional conventions, and even single generations consult only their own experience and knowledge in seeking to solve their problems, the answers they come up with are bound to be less complete, less effective, and less suited to the character and dispositions of the people called to live under them, than the answers that have grown up over generations of hard and careful and controlled experimentation that values the affection in which the tried and true and familiar are held by the population. To reject out of hand the traditional and the customary and rely only on your own mind and knowledge is not to make your decisions more rational (in the sense that decisions based on a larger amount of proven knowledge are more rational than ones based on less knowledge) but rather less so. This contrast between the "grown" and the "invented" is the key one we need to understand.

If this seems impossibly abstract, let me try and bring it down to earth with the following chicken-and-egg analogy. Which came first: the ordinary speaker of English (or indeed any other natural language) or the grammarian? The rationalist cast of mind is always on the lookout for first or definitional principles by which to judge specific performances or utterances or institutions. There is no more withering criticism in the rationalist lexicon than "what you're doing is not perfectly internally logical and consistent." In that case, the answer to which came first must be "the grammarian." Grammarians define the rules of proper speech based on logic and reason, and individual utterances are judged against that standard. Moreover, grammarians are the ones who continually push us to get rid of outmoded usages, inconsistent spellings, etc.

But language was not invented by grammarians. It grew; it grew out of the blooming, buzzing confusion of attempts by generations of people to communicate with each other. To do so successfully, they needed to develop certain regularities in the way they talked. Language simply *is* the existence of these established and shared regularities. After the fact, the grammarians came along and were able to tease out those regularities, to describe them and give them names, which we rather inaccurately refer to as the "rules" of grammar. But the grammarians did not invent language. Grammarians are the product of language and not the other way around. Moreover, all attempts to extirpate from language all the irregularities and contradictions, to abandon "grown" language and replace it with "invented" and wholly "rational" languages based on first principles, such as Esperanto, have been abject failures, certainly when measured by the number of people who speak them. The traditionalist understands that language *grows* in the tension between the search for rules, on the one hand, and the constantly evolving circumstances and experiences of native speakers that the rules can never fully capture and fix for all time, on the other hand. Natural grown language will always be richer, more subtle, and more elusive than is dreamt of in the philosophy of rationalist grammarians and the inventors of rational languages no one speaks.

If that example doesn't help, try this one: A professor I knew told me that in the U.S. Midwest there were two universities built near one another at roughly the same time. In the first, the rationalist planners designed a campus that looked spectacular from the air, with lovely landscaping and curving pathways that gave the whole a pleasing aspect … at least it was pleasing in theory. The problem was that in order to make pathways that looked good and orderly from thirty thousand feet, they had to follow routes that were inconvenient and awkward for those on the ground who were using them to try and get to where they needed to go, *which is actually the purpose of pathways*. The result was that people abandoned the paths and tramped across the lawns, creating pathways that were less pleasing to look at but actually got them where they wanted to go. The campus became a battleground between authorities trying to get people to respect their utopian but impractical "first principles" or "invented" design and the students who were late and needed to get to class.

The other campus, which was under the authority of traditionalists, took a different tack. They built their buildings but held off landscaping for a year or two so that they could observe where students actually wanted to go and the paths that they trod to get there. Once the paths were well established, the university simply paved them over and landscaped around them. The result was not so nice to look at from the air — about which the college authorities cared not a whit — but resulted in a harmonious relationship between those authorities and the students who were trying to get from their dorm to the lecture hall and then the cafeteria. Put another way, the pathways on the campus "grew" out of the needs and experiences of those who had to use them.

So rationalist inventors try to impose their will on the world, which they feel must give up its stubborn attachment to the old and the conventional and acquiesce to the dictates of what they think of as "reason." To their mind, human society is a machine, and its operation can always be tweaked by pulling on the right lever, improving the information technology, or installing a higher-performance valve. And if the whole machine is clapped out from age and use, it can be replaced with a new "high-performance" model that improves productivity. The fact that people loved the look or feel or sound of the old machine is mere sentimentality that must be ignored in the name of a higher social good. The world, and people, are simply the passive raw material on which abstract reason must leave its impression. And if the cost of a new machine is only the destruction of the attachment to and affection for tradition of which Oakeshott spoke so movingly, why, that is no cost at all, for what is the value of mere sentiment or, worse, prejudice, compared to the glories of a logical and well-designed contraption? You can't stop progress, eh!

"Gardeners" is the name I give to those who think of society more as a garden than a machine. For them, grown institutions are, on the whole, more effective and held in higher esteem than invented ones. Gardeners are by their nature mindful that they are not in total control. They are participants and not masters. They must make their peace with the effects of climate, of weather, of soil, of nutrients, and of the life cycle and characteristics of the plants they seek to cultivate. Gardeners know that they can create the conditions in which a garden will flourish, but they cannot overmaster the natural processes on which they depend; you cannot make flowers grow faster by pulling on them. In human terms, this means that while gardeners of institutions apply reason to their work, they must reason knowing the nature of their raw material and its behaviour under different conditions and, more importantly, the limits of their power to shape the world closer to their heart's desire.

Coming back to monarchy vs. republicanism, the two casts of mind I have described (what I will call the gardeners and the inventors) differ on the wellsprings of authority in political institutions. The rationalist inventors will tend to be of the view that institutions derive their legitimacy from their conformity to some set of abstract first principles; such as, say, that all authority derives from the people. The worth of institutions will be judged by how closely they hew to such foundational statements of principle. The traditionalist gardener, by contrast, will be of the view that human action does not proceed from abstract first principles, but from messy and very untheoretical practical experience of what works and has passed the test of time regardless of how it appears to those who value only first principles and not practical success.

Those of you who care about such things will find this distinction redolent of Max Weber, who argued that there were three potential sources of authority (in other words, three reasons why people might feel bound to obey the decisions of their rulers): custom and prescription, charismatic authority, and legal-rational authority of the type where people obey the law because they believe in the principles on which authority may be exercised. Let's set aside the charismatic form of authority for now, because it is extremely rare and dangerous, although we may come back to it because it is far more likely, in my humble opinion, to emerge in republics than in monarchies.

For now, let us be content to say that the other two forms of authority fit nicely with the two casts of mind I drew from Oakeshott. The traditionalist gardeners are drawn to monarchy that has grown out of custom and has become hallowed by the passage of time; the institution's worth has been proven by the continued willingness of people to live under it even if it might fail some "first principles" test. Rationalist inventors are drawn to the republican model, precisely because it sweeps away the distractions, incoherencies, and cobwebs of the past and allows people to live under institutions they have freely chosen and to whose foundational principles they subscribe. To revert to my language example, this is the difference between those who celebrate slowly evolving "usage" as the source of the genius of language, and those who are strict and inflexible grammarians who believe that native speakers' attachment to "uncorrected" traditional inconsistencies is a failing of the first order.

In the rest of this essay, I ask the question as to how we might choose between these two different and, in their own ways, quite legitimate approaches. In particular, I am going to put to you the case for monarchy and the Crown addressed to the rationalist.

I would start by observing that it is quite incorrect to take as the foundational principle of a democracy such as Canada's the idea that all authority derives from the people or from some written constitution approved by them. Indeed, the political and institutional history of the British parliamentary

tradition from which we emerged is that there has always been an active in-
itiating power, which is counterbalanced by a need to bring the population
along. As Leo Amery put it in his *Thoughts on the Constitution*:

> From William [the Conqueror's] day onwards the key to
> our constitutional evolution is to be found in the inter-
> action between the Crown, i.e. the central governing,
> directing and initiating element in the national life, and
> the nation in its various "estates," i.e. classes and com-
> munities, as the guardian of its written and unwritten laws
> and customs. The ambitions or needs of the Crown con-
> tinually demanded changes in the law which the nation
> was only prepared to accept after discussion or parley with
> its representatives and on terms. Out of that parley, pro-
> gressively more continuous and more intimate as needs
> increased, and out of those terms, grew our system, as we
> know it, of Government in and with Parliament, subject
> to the ever increasing influence of public opinion and to
> periodic review by the nation as a whole.

Note that in this view the Crown does not have derivative authority,
but rather original authority, authority in its own right, as the active element of the constitution that identifies and pursues national objectives. It
does not get this authority as a gift from the population. (The population
now gets to decide who *exercises* this power and for what purposes, but that
is a different matter.)

And out of the interplay between Crown and Parliament, and the need
for the first to obtain the consent of the second for its plans, grew a quite
unintended (or "grown") consequence, namely, that the personal rule of the
wearer of the crown was increasingly hemmed in by the requirements of
consent from Parliament to the government's ambitions. Without it being
our intention, or our plan, or our design (which is to say this result was not
"invented" by anyone, but it grew out of the genius of our lived experience),
the result has been to take power out of the hands of the sovereign and
place it in the hands of ministers of the Crown, who act in the sovereign's

name but themselves take responsibility for the actions of the state. Thus the politically accountable institution of the Crown has emerged as by far the greatest and most important part of the monarchy that once rested in the hands of the individual who occupied the throne.

The residual part of the monarchy, the person of the monarch himself or herself, now embodies the principle that the sovereign reigns but does not rule. This has enabled the "grown" emergence of a monarch above the political fray, who is untainted by partisan controversy and contention, who symbolizes in his or her person the unity of the nation beyond mere political disputes. I would be so bold to say that in an era of identity politics in which the political parties seem ever more bound to try and appeal to voters based on their membership in some group or another, whether taxpayers or sexual or racial minorities or veterans or the "middle class," such a unifying symbolism is sorely needed. Moreover, it cannot be supplied by a figure who emerges from the very political class that thrives on such division. In many republics (which are "invented" political institutions par excellence), criticism of the president is tantamount to treason, or at least has the flavour of *lèse-majesté*, and this institutional arrangement inevitably clothes mere political leadership in the dignity and glory of the symbols of national existence.

Moreover, fixed terms objectively make presidents less accountable than prime ministers, who may fall at any time (Jean Chrétien, a personally successful prime minister, was driven from office not by an election but by the loss of support of his own caucus) without its endangering in any way the continuity of the state or of national life, embodied in the Crown and the person of the monarch. This is, no doubt, one of the key reasons why, as Frank Buckley has richly documented, monarchy of the Canadian and British type is empirically connected with higher degrees of political freedom and lower degrees of corruption than presidential regimes around the world.

I would also submit that the hereditary principle is essential to the success of any enterprise aiming to remove partisan politics from the person of the head of state. No political process is required to identify and recruit the monarch, although it is now well established that the monarch sits on the throne only with the consent of Parliament (in the United Kingdom) or of Ottawa and the provinces in the case of Canada; so it is quite wrong to think of the monarch as some kind of imposition over which we have no control or influence. I can quote no less an authority on this nationally unifying theme than former prime minister Lester Pearson, who said in Parliament:

> The crown under the monarchical principle also lends, I think, stability and dignity to our national life, and I am sure that we all agree that that is important in a democratic system based on the free and active play of party controversies. The crown as head of the state and as represented in our country standing above all such controversies, commanding and deserving the respect and loyalty and affection of us all, ensures a more solid and secure foundation for national development than might otherwise be the case under some other form of democratic government.

This nationally unifying aspect of our "grown" monarchy is reinforced by the institution of the governor general (who, since the early 1950s, has invariably been a Canadian), endowed with virtually all the powers of the Queen but in addition enjoying powers she does not enjoy within Canada. I would submit that this helps to underline the extent to which the monarchy is an institution whose importance and complexity far transcends the person who happens to sit on the throne at any one moment. And while our celebrity-obsessed world may be fixated on the person of the monarch and the members of her family, the importance, the strength, and the flexibility of the monarchy extend far beyond and exceed vastly in importance the question of who the monarch may be at any particular time. Of course our Elizabethan era has been a golden age of monarchy because of the incomparable commitment of the Queen to her duty and her strength and dignity of character, but the monarchy will be no less vital and desirable under her son or grandson regardless of their personal virtues or foibles.

It is sometimes said that in the Canadian context the unifying symbolism of the Crown is vitiated by the existence of Quebec, for whom the monarchy is a mysterious holdover from the Conquest and British domination. There may be some small truth to this, but it ignores several other important truths equally worthy of our attention. First, I have carefully underlined the entirely changeable and evolving nature of any traditional or customary institution, whether monarchy, or language, or any other. It can evolve in positive and negative ways. In the case of the relationship between Quebec and the Crown, for generations the Crown was seen as the guarantor of the rights of the French and the Catholics in British North America against both the revolutionary Protestant zeal of the new American republic and the simmering hostility of the growing English-speaking and predominantly Protestant population of what was to become Canada. Indeed, one of the chief grievances of the American revolutionaries was the *Quebec Act*, which sought to embody and protect, as a matter of imperial policy, the rights of the French and Catholics in the New World. When invited to join in the American Revolution, Quebeckers vastly preferred to remain under the Crown.

The hostility of Quebec to the monarchy, to the extent that it truly exists, is itself the product of a decades-long effort to rewrite history by Quebec nationalists and it will surely not be the last such questioning of history and the monarchy in that province. Who knows what the future holds for the monarchy and its place in the affections of Quebeckers? If the past is any guide, such opinions are wildly changeable.

And against the alleged hostility of Quebec toward the monarchy must be weighed the attitudes and feelings of, say, Indigenous Canadians toward the Crown, especially in an era when "reconciliation" is the watchword heard from every tongue. Like French Catholics, Indigenous people historically have treasured the fact that their relationship with the newcomers was defined in written and unwritten agreements with the Crown, embodied in the person of the monarch. Constant appeals by Indigenous leaders to Buckingham Palace in seeking to vindicate their rights is proof positive, in my view, that the monarchy is again coming into its own as a vital symbol of unity we can ill afford to dispense with. The greatest monarchists of all in Canada today, in my estimation, are Indigenous people.

I do not believe, however, that this unifying symbolism exhausts in any way the symbolic value of the Queen, nor the justification for Canada sharing a royal family with a number of other realms in the Commonwealth. Chief among these other symbolic values is this: because the position of monarch has "grown" out of a long constitutional struggle to tame the hitherto untrammelled powers of the king, all of us over whom Elizabeth reigns are reminded by the institution of *our* monarchy that we emerge from a shared tradition of the rule of law, of the indispensable consent of the governed, of Magna Carta, habeas corpus, and a thousand other rights and traditions and customs that have been successfully transplanted to lands far from the place where the original struggles occurred and which nonetheless gave us these inestimable blessings. Why we should respect and show deference, as we are constantly exhorted to do, to the authority of, say, soulless "invented" international organizations, such as the United Nations, dominated by thuggish regimes and tinpot dictators who share few of our values, but be embarrassed by our embrace of an international monarchy that gracefully embodies values from which our society sprang and whose enduring worth we should celebrate every day, is a mystery I shall never solve.

But, the rationalist republican "inventor" will inevitably argue, why stick with some hoary old "grown" relic from the past that, no matter what its dwindling list of virtues, could surely be improved upon? Let us put our heads together and invent a rational alternative that eliminates the many defects while preserving the few remaining virtues of monarchy.

This is where we come face to face with the very real limitations of an inventor's rationalism fixated on reason alone applied to the present, rather than on a gardener's reason applied to experience that has stood the test of time. For while rationalists like to think that reason honestly applied leads all rational people to the same conclusion, in fact nothing is further from the truth. Far from being a unifying act, trying to invent a "purely Canadian" head of state will lead reasonable people of good will to reach completely different conclusions about what we should do. Even people who might not like monarchy will, in those circumstances, often prefer to stick with what they know, even if it does not inspire them with enthusiasm. John Fraser, in an article for the Macdonald-Laurier Institute's flagship publication, *Inside Policy*, has rightly observed that this is exactly what happened in Australia. He reminds us that

> in 1999, a referendum was held in a country [Australia] that
> is our closest constitutional cousin, even closer than Britain

actually. It is also a country where opinion polls, those limited and often faulty dried chicken bones of today's High Oracles of a nation's mood, clearly showed Australians were ready to ditch their version of the Crown. What happened? When it came time to say aye or nay, it was clear that Australians didn't fancy any more power going into the hands of an already too-powerful-by-a-half, democratically elected, federal prime minister. It turned out that the Australian Crown would do quite nicely, after all.

That the rationalist will perhaps be offended by the notion that we might stay with what we know because it is *good enough* despite its defects and is superior, taken in the round, to any realistic and practical alternative, should not trouble us in the least. Remember that republics are often born out of revolution, which by definition sweeps away the established order. If you have driven the old regime out, you have the "advantage," if I can call it that, of not being able to keep it, and you *must* "invent" something new.

Canada, which has enjoyed the inestimable benefit of growing slowly and peacefully without revolutionary interruption, has been able to maintain the tradition of authority flowing from custom and prescription (and the attachment and affection that engenders) while modernizing it through the evolution of parliamentary government in a way that is the envy of the world. And if the Australian experience is anything to go by, the result is a system that works admirably and to which no more acceptable alternative has yet been proposed.

Some (mostly the rationalist inventors among us) find this a deplorable state of affairs. I am not among them, for I am a gardener. I applaud a country whose arrangements for head of state are not the object of political contention, but are widely acquiesced in and work well; that place the symbolism of the dignity and unity of the state beyond the realm of narrow partisan manoeuvring; that proudly display for all to see the scars and remnants of past struggles to end arbitrary rule and protect and honour traditional rights; and that symbolically remind politicians every day that they are not our masters, but indeed are the servants of something far greater than they.

Heritage and Innovation:

The Future Reign of Charles III*

David Johnson

W e are living within the final act of the Second Elizabethan Era. At some point in the next decade or so Elizabeth II will pass from this Earth, bringing to a close the longest reign of a monarch in English and British history. At the very instant the Queen's life ends, and barring a tragedy befalling the Prince of Wales between now and then, Charles will ascend to the throne, automatically possessing all the rights, titles, powers, privileges, duties, and obligations of a sovereign of the United Kingdom and the Commonwealth realms. And the words will be said: "The Queen is dead; long live the King."

In the days and weeks following the death of Elizabeth II, we will see an uptick in popular support for the monarchy. This will likely be registered in public opinion polling in the United Kingdom, Canada, and

---

* Some brief passages in this article previously appeared in David Johnson, *Battle Royal: Monarchists vs. Republicans and the Crown of Canada* (Toronto: Dundurn, 2018).

other Commonwealth realms, and within other countries worldwide. During this time people will be presented with blanket media coverage of her funeral (already planned and organized under the operational name London Bridge). We will all be recipients of copious media stories dealing with her life and times, her historic reign, her role in the transition of the British Empire into a Commonwealth, and her legacy of service and duty to her Crown and her peoples. There will be many tears shed as we are reminded of the majestic royal titan now departed. It will also be noted, by monarchists, that one of Elizabeth's great legacies to her realms is that she ensured, despite decades of turmoil and criticism, that there would be a strong and viable Crown to pass on to her son.

Yet this period of transition also will be marked by complaint and ridicule as republican critics of the monarchy will question why we still have an ancient and, to them, archaic monarchy in these countries in the thoroughly modern twenty-first century. How is it, republicans will ask, that we can call ourselves a democracy when the head of state of these countries is a hereditary monarch? With specific reference to this country, the leadership of Citizens for a Canadian Republic will challenge us to wonder why our head of state is an English aristocrat? Why he must be an Anglican? Why can no Canadian ever aspire to head of state? And why should Canada continue to have the institution of monarchy in this country — an institution, to republicans, that is elitist, anti-democratic, and a reminder of our colonialist past as part of the racist and militarist British Empire?

If we are to be a modern, multicultural, and egalitarian democracy, republicans will stress, surely it's time that we abolish the monarchy in this country, becoming a truly independent nation. Very early on into the new reign of Charles III[1] we will also likely hear concerns and complaints from many Canadians wondering why we don't get to vote on whether we want Charles as our King. Or whether we could choose Prince William as our King over Charles?

Why is it, some people will ask, that we cannot have a national referendum on whether we even want to maintain the monarchy in Canada? Some letter writers to newspapers will likely assert that the ideal time to hold such a referendum is between the death of the Queen and before the coronation, when Charles becomes King.

Republican criticism will soon turn to scorn and anger when they learn about the laws of succession, the instantaneous accession to the throne, and the fact that, while in Canada it is perfectly possible to abolish the institution of the monarchy in this country, such action requires a constitutional amendment rooted to the unanimous consent of the federal government and Parliament and all ten provincial governments and legislative assemblies. Absent such an amendment, the monarchy will continue in this country in perpetuity. Monarchy is a natural default mode within the written Canadian Constitution, much to the chagrin of republicans.

Looking Ahead: The Future Reign of Charles III

So this we know as monarchists, as we look ahead to the inevitable and sad passing of Elizabeth II: the institution of the monarchy will continue. Charles will become King (it is highly unlikely that he would abdicate in favour of his eldest son, Prince William, Duke of Cambridge). In this country, public opinion will be divided between monarchists, who support the succession and the new sovereign; republicans, who will mock and ridicule the monarchy, calling for its abolition; and many other Canadians existing in the mushy middle between these two well-established sides in this perennial debate. Those in this middle ground may or may not express support for monarchism or republicanism, depending on the circumstances and whether they like or dislike the current royals.

What will the future reign of Charles III look like? We already know some of the contours of the years to come in the life and times of King Charles. At his coronation not only will he be crowned, separately, as King of the United Kingdom, Canada, and the other Commonwealth realms, he will also be bestowed with the title of Defender of the Faith, making him the supreme governor of the Church of England. He will be called upon to swear to maintain the Church of Scotland. And, given the unanimous decision at the 2018 Commonwealth Heads of Government Meeting (CHOGM) in London, England, Charles will enter his reign bearing the title, among others, of Head of the Commonwealth.

The Church of England will be the first institution to notice a change with the new sovereign and supreme governor. While Charles will swear, at his coronation, to be "Defender of the Faith," he will likely stress, at this time or soon thereafter, that he also sees his religious role as being a "defender of faiths." To Catherine Mayer, a biographer of Prince Charles, he is a devout if somewhat mystical Anglican who sees the important interconnections of faith, spiritualism, and the divine in all the world's great religions and who wishes to build harmony and respect among these pillars of devotion. "In Charles," writes Mayer, "the Church of England stands to gain a Supreme Governor who takes his duties, and his religion, exceptionally seriously."[2] These duties will be seen by King Charles III as much as promoting ecumenism and interfaith understanding and respect, especially between Christians, Jews, and Muslims, as advancing the spiritual life and applied "good works" of the Church of England.

The Commonwealth will not be far behind in feeling the influence of its new head and his immediate family. Just like his mother, Charles III will take his role as Head of the Commonwealth very seriously; indeed, he has already assumed a growing leadership role in this regard as the Queen's international travels have diminished. He will likely travel extensively throughout the Commonwealth, especially in the early years of his reign, attending Commonwealth conferences, and promoting its various programs of democratic development and good governance, socio-economic progress, education, health care, environmental protection, advocacy for the rights of women and girls, and the cause of youth empowerment. Given some lingering concerns about his own public popularity as well as that of his wife, Queen Camilla, he will also likely be advised to ask his sons and daughters-in-law — Prince William and Catherine, Duke and Duchess of Cambridge; and Prince Harry and Meghan, Duke and Duchess of Sussex — to tour the Commonwealth, to see and be seen, and to promote not only the ideals and practical benefits of the Commonwealth, but, by extension, the value of the monarchy and its royal leaders.

And what else will Charles do as King? The other causes he will champion, in his own royal way, will be those that have been of interest to him throughout his adult life. He will continue to promote his ideas and ideals of harmony in life. When occasions merit, he will speak of the importance of humanity being one with the Earth and our environment and the need for us to be better caretakers of nature and the ecology that supports all life on Earth. He will encourage us all to be more concerned about environmental protection, ecological conservation, sustainable development, and the importance of organic farming. He will also use his public appearances and speeches to talk about the dangers of poverty and social exclusion and the loss to societies when substantial numbers of people, especially youth, feel no connection to the broader society of which they are a part because they live on the margins of that society. He will talk about the significance of reaching out to and supporting youth at the very beginning of their adult lives, just as he will stress the need for societies to care for the elderly in the twilight years of their lives. And he will continue to speak in favour of social cohesion; the need for sound urban planning that respects the people, the environment, and the communities for whom such planning is designed; and the cultural significance of architecture that is in harmony with its natural and built surroundings.

His biographers, notably Jonathan Dimbleby,[3] Catherine Mayer, and Sally Bedell Smith,[4] confirm that Charles is a passionate man and these passions will not be eradicated once he assumes the throne. As King, however, he will not be as free to pursue his passions and his interests in the same fashion as when he was Prince of Wales. As King, he will be more circumscribed in his ability to act as an advocate for his causes, but as King he will also have access to certain levers of influence that only the sovereign possesses. When he becomes King, Charles will have to scrupulously adhere to the constitutional principle that the monarch is not to become involved in partisan matters of political debate, either in the United Kingdom or anywhere throughout the Commonwealth, or any other country, for that matter. In accordance with constitutional convention, the Crown is to be above politics.

Charles knows this, as did his mother and grandfather before him. But being nonpartisan does not mean that the sovereign is prohibited from speaking about the importance of broad moral and social principles. These principles address what it is to be good, to do good, and to promote goodness in society. So long as he speaks to these matters in general terms, dealing with values rather than specific governmental policies and programs, and refraining even from discussing certain principles when they are the subject matter of current partisan debates, Charles is free to encourage people to think more deeply about the societies in which they live and how we can work together, in harmony with our fellow human beings and our environment, to make these societies better.

Once Charles is King, it is likely that he will transfer the Prince's Trust to his sons, William and Harry, giving them the responsibilities of overseeing these charitable organizations while also providing them the opportunities to reorient the existing trust, or to create new ones, to address issues and concerns of interest to them. As King, Charles will lose the ability to be directly involved in the management and direction of these institutions, thus losing these venues for advancing his charitable ideas. But as one door closes, others open. As King, Charles will inherit the right to give the monarch's annual Christmas and Commonwealth Day messages. These addresses, written by the sovereign himself, without being subject to the advice of any British or Commonwealth first minister, will give Charles the opportunity to present his ideas to an international audience on the importance of these festive occasions and what lessons we should draw from them. As with his mother's addresses, his will likely speak to general matters respecting the importance of family and tradition, being generous and charitable, reaching out to others, and respecting the ideals for which the Commonwealth stands. Critics of these messages tend to dismiss them as mere "motherhood" statements; supporters will see them as expressions of "profound simplicities."

Perhaps most importantly for Charles, the kingship will place him in the position of hosting the weekly audience with the British prime minister when the British parliament is in session. These regular meetings will give Charles the opportunity to discuss, in strictest confidence, any and all affairs of state and matters of public policy that he may want to raise with the prime minister. Likewise, prime ministers will have the ability to sound out the King on policy and program ideas, gaining his advice, encouragement, or warnings on the course of public policies. Given his extensive international travels and his close connection to the Commonwealth, prime ministers will also likely speak to him of international affairs, seeking his guidance and input on various matters. Any advice proffered by the King to his prime minister, however, is just that, advice, which a prime minister may accept or not according to his or her discretion. Charles will have the formalized opportunity to present his ideas and concerns to the British head of government; but as with all his royal predecessors dating back to the eighteenth century, he will be subject to the rules of responsible government, whereby the democratically elected prime minister and government will be solely responsible for the development and administration of policies and programs, subject to the oversight of Parliament. As King and Head of the Commonwealth, Charles will also be in a position, during his travels, to meet with Commonwealth heads of government and their ministers and to discuss with them matters of public policy within their countries. Again, such discussions would be purely advisory, but they will present the King with the opportunity to raise matters of concern with these officials, confidentially encouraging and warning as he sees fit.

The Canadian Crown in the Twenty-First Century

The institution of monarchy is embedded within the Canadian constitution, meaning that upon the death of Elizabeth II the royal succession will occur in time-honoured tradition, Charles will become King, and the Canadian viceregents will carry on their work as they always have. There is a world of difference, however, between existing and thriving. While the monarchy undoubtedly has been existing in this country, in many ways it has been "merely" existing. Public opinion surveys over the past quarter-century have often found that a plurality if not an outright majority of respondents wish to see the monarchy abolished in this country, with a Canadian able to be selected, or better yet, elected as our head of state.[5] These surveys have also suggested that a clear majority of Canadians do not wish to see Prince Charles become our next King. Republican sentiment is strong among many Canadians, and past governments have picked up on this. Public and governmental support for the monarchy in Quebec is negligible, and past federal governments prior to that of Stephen Harper worked to downplay the role of the royal family in the life of Canada while seeking to elevate the status of the governor general as the de facto Canadian head of state. Royal visits to this country have become fewer, and shorter.

The hard reality to monarchists is that, as republican Michael Bliss long argued, to most young Canadians the monarchy is irrelevant, a useless anachronism that means nothing. Or, if it means anything, it is something to be laughed at and ridiculed.[6] The Crown is not cool. A symptom of this perception of irrelevance, and the lack of awareness flowing from it, is that most Canadians would be hard pressed to name the current governor general or their provincial lieutenant governor, and most Canadians would be unable to explain what the role of these viceregents is, what their reserve powers are, and how, when, and why these very real powers can still be exercised. For an institution that, to monarchists, is a fundamental pillar of our constitutional system and a vital link to our history and our political development as a liberal democracy, such apathy and ignorance are appalling. If the monarchy is of vital significance to Canadian history, our political development as a democratic people, and the ceremonial, social, educational, and charitable life of this country, then the monarchy should be a thriving institution, known and respected by Canadians. But it is not.

Are we destined to have to live with some of the worst fears of both republicans and monarchists: a monarchy that cannot be abolished but a Crown that is viewed by most Canadians as virtually useless, a meaningless yet embarrassing ornamental bauble that we would and should discard if we could? Or can we aspire to something better? If we know that the monarchy will continue in this country, can we have a better monarchy? One that actually connects to most Canadians and means something to them? Rather than having a monarchy that simply continues to exist, could we actually have a Crown that thrives in the future?

The Canadian Crown 2.0: The Continuing British Connection

What might a revitalized Canadian monarchy look like? And what would it take to achieve such a thing as a Crown that most Canadians would actually respect? In probing for an answer to these questions, a keyword rises to the fore: "more." If the monarchy is to be appreciated by most Canadians, if it is to be seen as important to the country and relevant to their lives, its representatives have to do more, and have to be seen to be doing more. Simply continuing with the status quo, with business as usual for the regal and viceregal powers that be, is simply a recipe for a monarchy existing in the social and political doldrums of irrelevancy, always vulnerable to public dissension and republican calls for abolition. If it is to be relevant to Canadians, the monarchy has to earn their respect, and it must do this by being a bigger part of their lives, and the lives of their communities, their province, and their country. Elizabeth II has long had a personal motto: "I must be seen to be believed."[7] This idea is central to any revitalization of the monarchy in Canada, and every representative of the Crown must play their part in such renewal, starting right at the top.

The future King and the royal family will be expected to do more, if the monarchy during the reign of Charles III is to strengthen its hold on the Canadian people. Charles will come to the throne knowing that his accession has been met with much criticism and outright hostility in Canada. He would be well advised to plan a royal tour of Canada at the earliest convenience, bringing his queen with him, and spending a fair amount of time in this country, travelling through it extensively, and meeting with people from the prime minister, premiers, Indigenous leaders, and heads of major charities, to ordinary Canadians involved in charitable work, schoolchildren, youth, veterans, and seniors. Prince William, the new Prince of Wales, and Catherine, Duchess of Cambridge, and other members of the royal family, especially Prince Harry and Meghan, Duke and Duchess of Sussex, should also be expected to regularly travel to this country, promoting their own and various Canadian philanthropic causes. If the royal family is to be appreciated by Canadians, they have to be seen by Canadians. But they also need to do more than simply be present here. Given that support for charitable and philanthropic work has become the heart of the social/ceremonial work of the monarchy and its representatives, the royals need to be more active in supporting such causes in Canada. The key here, perhaps, is the Prince's Trust Canada.

In 1976, Charles, Prince of Wales, established a charitable foundation in the United Kingdom with the name of the Prince's Trust. This organization was, and still is, designed to provide financial and practical support to young people aged thirteen to thirty who are in danger of dropping out of school or who are facing difficulties finding employment. The trust offers mentoring support to youth — both individually and in groups — with respect to their education. It also provides funding for twelve-week development courses designed to give participants job skills and workplace training, experience in collaborative group work and team problem-solving, and enhanced personal motivation. With an annual budget of some £59 million ($100 million) as of 2018, the trust has helped over a million young people since its inception, with over sixty-three thousand youth participating in its programming in 2018. And since 1976 it has provided seed money leading to the creation of over eighty thousand businesses. The Prince's trust has become one of Charles's signature charitable undertakings and one linking the royal family to the needs of some of Britain's most underprivileged people.[8] As David Starkey has argued, the demonstrated success rate of this trust is striking, "and politicians — New Labour and Newer Tories alike — strive to learn from it and emulate it." In assessing all of Charles's public policy interests, Starkey suggests they form the intellectual basis of the reign yet to be: "Here then is a new kingdom of the mind, spirit, culture and values which is not unworthy of a thousand-year-old throne."[9]

In 2011, the Prince of Wales expanded the international reach of his philanthropic works with the creation of the Prince's Charities Canada (renamed the Prince's Trust Canada in 2018), a registered Canadian charity designed to help some of the neediest persons in Canadian society. "I established the Prince's Trust Canada," the Prince of Wales has said, "so that I could connect the accomplishments of my charities in the U.K. and across the world with organizations in Canada in order to make a difference in the lives of Canadians."[10] The Prince's Trust Canada has three core objectives: providing entrepreneurship training for veterans of the Canadian Armed Forces and those in the process of transitioning from military to civilian life; assisting socio-economically disadvantaged young people gain valuable work experience, life skills, and personal confidence through youth employability programs; and promoting and helping Indigenous communities as they work to nurture, protect, and promote their native languages.

Since 2011, the Prince's Trust Canada has recorded some significant accomplishments as it has established itself and reached out to its target communities. It possesses a board of directors giving it demonstrated expertise in corporate management, policy and program development, and charitable outreach, and a staff experienced in all three of the Trust's core objectives. It also boasts an advisory council of prominent Canadians ranging from David Onley, former lieutenant governor of Ontario, serving as the chair; to Phillip Crawley, publisher of the *Globe and Mail*; Robert Ghiz, a former premier of Prince Edward Island; General (retired) Rick Hillier, a former Canadian chief of defence staff; Audrey McLaughlin, former leader of the New Democratic Party of Canada; and Nathan Tidridge, teacher and constitutional expert.

Most importantly, the trust has already made its presence felt. It has partnered with Indigenous organizations to publish children's books written in a variety of Indigenous languages, including Cree, Dene, Lakota, Ojibwe, and Inuktitut. It piloted a number of "Get Into" cohorts early in its institutional life, with these groups giving young people the opportunity to get relevant work experience through employment programs developed by employers to address skills shortages in specific employment sectors. Early data indicates that eight in ten participating young persons are eventually hired by participating employers. As of 2018, some fourteen cohorts were planned for Calgary, Winnipeg, and the Greater Toronto Area. And, for veterans and service personnel transitioning out of the military, the trust has created a variety of programs to provide practical business and entrepreneurial skills, knowledge, and advice. Programs here range from seven-day entrepreneurial "bootcamps"; to one-day workshops; to ongoing coaching support for veterans creating their own start-up firms, with such support running from business planning, operational strategizing, to pro bono legal support.

Just as with the Prince's Trust in the United Kingdom, the Prince's Trust Canada has made a name for itself in the realm of Canadian charitable good works in just a few years. As we look ahead to the reign of Charles III, this trust, under the leadership of the new Prince of Wales, Prince William, can and should be expected to do more in its established fields of socio-economic support, while possibly even branching out to new, different, yet needed initiatives. It is not hard to envisage such a trust expanding its outreach to include such matters as the integration of new immigrants into Canadian society; linking young Canadians in need of job experience with seniors' facilities needing volunteers and workers to interact and socialize with seniors; and partnering with such organizations as Habitat for Humanity and local community historical and architectural preservation societies to save, preserve, and renovate dilapidated and threatened local heritage buildings for future use as low-cost housing and other community, charity, and local-business uses.

The Prince's Trust Canada has an established track record, proven professional leadership, and a strong and stable institutional presence. If the Prince's Trust Canada did not yet exist, monarchists looking for a means by which the presence and role of the monarchy could be enhanced in Canada during the future reign of Charles III would likely call for the establishment of such a trust, playing a role already pioneered in the United Kingdom. That such a trust already exists in Canada is testament to the visionary wisdom of Prince Charles; that such a trust could do much more to build upon the foundations already established by the Prince of Wales is for the future Prince of Wales, his advisors, the board of directors of the Prince's Trust Canada, and Canadian viceregents to contemplate.

The Canadian Crown 2.0: The Viceregents' Connection

That last sentence bears reflection. If the monarchy is to be revitalized in Canada during the reign of Charles III, the bulk of this work will fall to the Canadian viceregents — governors general and lieutenant governors. These are the officials representing the Crown in this country on a daily basis, performing the official and ceremonial work of the monarchy nationwide and in each province. They are the ones who can make the most difference to the stature of the monarchy if they want to, and if they are supported in this task by their respective governments, because they are closest, and most visible, to their people. If you have to be seen to be believed, these are the ones who most need to be seen. Once again we confront the word "more."

On a basic level they will have to do more of what they are already doing: more social engagements; more school, university, and hospital visits; more meetings with community and business groups; more speeches to service clubs and charities; and, consequently, more travel throughout their jurisdictions. In this work they would be well advised to focus attention on causes and charities promoting the interests of young Canadians and students, new Canadians, immigrants, multicultural groups, Indigenous Canadians and their socio-economic and educational needs, environmental groups concerned with conservation and sustainable development, and local community groups involved in such matters as building social capital, heritage conservation, and community revitalization projects. All these matters are important, and always in need of official recognition and sponsorship. These concerns, and many others, are also matters that many Canadians are interested in, devoting their own time and money in the quest for making a positive difference to their local, regional, and national community. Involvement with, and support for, such interests would provide the viceregents with noble causes for which they could make their own contributions to the social good of Canada and its provinces, while also having the benefit of getting the viceregents seen by more and more people and known for their allegiance to Canadians from all walks of life who are intent on making Canada a better place to live.

On a different and newer level, moreover, the viceregents can be encouraged to elevate their work, becoming more innovative and effective advocates of philanthropy designed to promote Canadian culture, heritage, and social interests both nationally and provincially. Here, the Canadian viceregents can take a lesson from Charles and the work of the Prince's Trust Canada. Governors in the past have been good at inaugurating honours and awards such as the Governor General's Caring Canadian Award, the Governor General's History Award for Excellence in Teaching, the Lieutenant Governor's Ontario Heritage Award, the Lieutenant Governor's Award for Excellence in British Columbia Wines, and the Lieutenant Governor's Persons with Disabilities Employer Partnership Award (Nova Scotia). What most have not done, however, is use their good offices to establish trusts to promote select and worthy causes both nationally and provincially.

One notable exception is the Rideau Hall Foundation (RHF), established in 2012 under the leadership of then Governor General David Johnston. This organization, a registered Canadian charity, is designed to link the Office of the Governor General with a host of other philanthropic partner organizations all sharing a vision to "connect, honour, and inspire Canadians."[11] The foundation focuses its activities around four themes: learning, leadership, innovation, and giving. In 2017 the foundation reported revenues of $11.8 million and accumulated assets of $28.4 million. In that year 90 percent of total expenses of $12.9 million were devoted to foundation programming and grants and scholarships.[12] Operational activities supported by this funding spanned the foundation's themes: $5.8 million for the Queen Elizabeth Scholars Program designed to promote both young Canadian university students and postgraduates continuing their studies abroad, while also assisting similar Commonwealth and international scholars to study within Canadian postsecondary institutions; funding support for the Learning Partnership for Indigenous Youth and Imagine a Canada, a national youth-based arts initiative established by the National Centre for Truth and Reconciliation; the promotion of the national Giving Behaviour Project, a study of Canadians' philanthropic behaviours and interests; and programs designed to foster a culture of Canadian innovation, including the establishment of an Innovation Advisory Committee to assist the RHF in this future work.[13]

Through these, and many other programs and initiatives, big and small, the Rideau Hall Foundation serves to bring Canadians together around its four themes, to promote fundraising and charitable giving for its projects, and to provide valuable and meaningful support to Canadians involved in learning and education; leadership and volunteering; social, scientific, and cultural innovation; and charitable giving. In many ways the RHF plays a convening role long advocated by the Prince of Wales. Such specialized policy and programming through such a charitable foundation are new to the role of the Office of the Governor General, yet fully in keeping with the traditional philanthropic role that governors general have always played in the history of Canada. The Rideau Hall Foundation shows how the viceregal role and function can be subject to innovation and creative development serving primarily to advance the well-being of Canadians but also promoting the bond between Crown and country and showing Canadians how and why viceregal activities actually benefit Canada and Canadians in the "real world." In this manner the RHF is leading the way in illustrating to all those interested in the work of viceregents — monarchists, governments, parliamentarians, the media, and interested citizens — how viceregents can do more to rejuvenate the institutions of the monarchy in this country.

Can provincial lieutenant governors aspire to follow the lead of the Office of the Governor General? Aspire, yes; but replicate the organizational structure and breadth of programming of the Rideau Hall Foundation, probably not. Scale and resources do matter. To date three provinces (British Columbia, Alberta, and Saskatchewan) have established foundations for their Government Houses, but only the Government House Foundation in British Columbia supports the ongoing charitable work of the lieutenant governor. (The purpose of the other two organizations is limited to the support and maintenance of the respective Government Houses. Alberta's is now a government conference centre, while that of Saskatchewan accommodates the viceregal office, a museum, and meeting space.) Provincial viceregal offices in Manitoba, Nova Scotia, and Newfoundland and Labrador in past decades have contemplated the creation of such foundations, but no actions have been forthcoming. The time and effort and cost of launching such a foundation would serve as an obvious impediment to such a reform, especially in smaller provinces where viceregal offices possess total staff complements of between three and eight persons. Political optics may also militate against provincial viceregents following this course of action. It is not hard to imagine mainstream public opinion in Quebec being critical of any move by the lieutenant governor of Quebec to seek to elevate the role of the viceregent, and the monarchy, in that province. It is also possible that certain premiers, cabinet ministers, and their advisors might question any new, or even the perception of any new, public monies going to support these new viceregal foundations, the types of charities they might support, and the propriety of lieutenant governors engaging in fundraising for select and hence privileged charities. When confronted with courses of action that require additional time and effort and money, one easy and cautious option is always to maintain the status quo.

But does this mean that significant viceregal innovation to elevate the role of the monarchy in Canada will be restricted to the federal order of government? No. The Office of the Governor General and the Rideau Hall Foundation seek to promote the philanthropic goals of the foundation by bringing "diverse partners together from various sectors and regions to co-create solutions employing a range of partnership tools."[14] Why could not provincial viceregents and their offices be "partners" in certain initiatives? The RHF's current focus on education and learning, promoting leadership, fostering charitable giving, and enhancing cultures of innovation are subjects of philanthropic interest in all ten provinces, with lieutenant governors and their offices likely able to find local, provincial initiatives worthy of support through combined RHF–lieutenant governor initiatives. There is no legal or constitutional impediment preventing the Office of the Governor General and the Rideau Hall Foundation from co-operating, working in tandem, or partnering with particular offices of lieutenant governors with respect to shared interests and projects having both national and provincial appeal. In certain instances, such co-operation may be loose, more focused on shared public relations and public communications highlighting RHF initiatives in given provinces; in other cases, co-operation may be tighter and more organized, with the RHF partnering closely with provincial viceregents in bringing certain projects and events to life. Regardless of the depth of engagement between the two viceregal sides, such co-operation would serve to elevate the role and stature of both sets of viceregents while also broadening general public awareness of the presence of monarchy in the everyday life of Canadians. In this sense, greater co-operation in philanthropic endeavours shared between the federal and provincial viceregents can be a "force multiplier" for the promotion of monarchy in this country.

The Canadian Crown 2.0: Royals and Canadians

The greatest "force multiplier" is yet to be addressed. If we wish to see a revitalized and more vibrant monarchy in Canada during the reign of Charles III, and if greater co-operation between the Office of the Governor General and those of provincial lieutenant governors can be a means to that end, then we should think about bringing the Prince's Trust Canada into this policy and program equation. If it is possible for federal and provincial viceregents to work together on shared projects of mutual interest, then it should also be possible for both sets of viceregents to establish co-operative and mutually beneficial working relationships with the Prince's Trust Canada. The three current key priorities of the Prince's Trust Canada — promoting entrepreneurial training for Canadian veterans and service personnel transitioning to civilian life, helping young Canadians build employability skills and experience, and assisting Indigenous communities in protecting and promoting their Indigenous languages — are all priorities that any Canadian viceregent would be happy to promote and support. Again, from general public relations and communications activities to identification of needs and possible beneficiaries of support to more specific operational support in program implementation, Canadian viceregents and their offices could play a variety of important roles in assisting the Prince's Trust Canada in fulfilling its goals. Indeed, through such greater co-operation and shared service, all these actors in the realm of the practical application of monarchy in Canada could do more, and be seen to be doing more. We have the agents, the tools, and the methods. It is just a matter of how we use them, creatively, intelligently, and progressively. Lieutenant governors could be seen working with the governor general to advance Rideau Hall Foundation good works. The governor general and the Rideau Hall Foundation could be witnessed co-operating with and sharing in the promotion of noble charitable activities with lieutenant governors in the provinces. And all Canadian viceregents could share in collaborations with the Prince's Trust Canada, and stride figurative and real stages with the likes of Prince William and Catherine, Duke and Duchess of Cambridge; Prince Harry and Meghan, Duke and Duchess of Sussex; and King Charles and Queen Camilla. This is star power indeed, a glittering, revitalized Crown for a new reign.

Notes

1. I make the presumption that Charles will retain this given name as King. At the time of his accession, of course, he may choose another name as his reigning given name, possibly George, in honour of his grandfather. My presumption for "Charles" is based on nothing more than my own gut feeling.

2. Catherine Mayer, *Charles: The Heart of a King* (London: WH Allen, 2015), 343.

3. Jonathan Dimbleby, *The Prince of Wales: A Biography* (New York: William Morrow, 1994).

4. Sally Bedell Smith, *Prince Charles: The Passions and Paradoxes of an Improbable Life* (New York: Random House, 2017).

5. David Johnson, *Battle Royal: Monarchists vs. Republicans and the Crown of Canada* (Toronto: Dundurn, 2018), 153–57.

6. Ibid., 247.

7. Rebecca Davis, "Sixty Years Later, Queen Elizabeth II Still Reigns," *Daily Maverick*, February 6, 2012, dailymaverick.co.za/article/2012-02 -06-sixty-years-later-queen-elizabeth-still-reigns/#VW82UUbbLIU.

8. Mayer, *Charles,* 179–88; Dimbleby, *The Prince of Wales*, 235–41; Prince's Trust, *Prince's Trust Group Annual Report*, 2018, princes-trust. org.uk/about-the-trust/research-policies-reports/annual-report.

9. David Starkey, *Crown and Country: The Kings and Queens of England: A History* (London: HarperPress, 2004), 500.

10. "About Us," Prince's Trust Canada, princestrust.ca/about-us.

11. "About," Rideau Hall Foundation, rhf-frh.ca/about.

12. Rideau Hall Foundation, *2017 Annual Report*, 2018, 12–13, rhf-frh. ca/wp-content/uploads/2018/08/RHF_AnnualReport.pdf.

13. Ibid., 6–10.

14. Ibid., 5.

CONTRIBUTORS

National Chief Perry Bellegarde, SOM

Perry Bellegarde has served in several elected leadership positions in First Nations governments. He was elected National Chief of the Assembly of First Nations in 2014 and re-elected in 2018. Originally from Little Black Bear First Nation in Treaty 4 Territory, he has spent thirty years putting into practice his strong beliefs in the laws and traditions instilled in him by many chiefs and elders. In 2018, the Province of Saskatchewan recognized him with its highest honour, the Saskatchewan Order of Merit. National Chief Bellegarde remains committed to building on the momentum created since his first election. His national platform and agenda, Closing the Gap, have directly influenced the federal government's planning and priorities.

Brian Lee Crowley

Brian Lee Crowley is managing director of the Macdonald-Laurier Institute. Dr. Crowley was also the founder of the Atlantic Institute for Market Studies (AIMS) in Halifax, one of the country's leading regional think tanks. Dr. Crowley has distinguished himself as an accomplished author, a former Clifford Clark Visiting Economist with the federal Department of Finance, and as a frequent media commentator with expertise related to Canada–U.S. relations, foreign affairs, natural resources and public finances, regional development policy, and health care.

The Honourable Judith Guichon, OBC

Judith Guichon served as the twenty-ninth lieutenant governor of British Columbia from 2012 to 2018. Prior to this appointment she owned and operated a ranch in the Nicola Valley in the British Columbia interior. She served as a director for the Fraser Basin Council of British Columbia, a director of the Grasslands Conservation Council of B.C., and member of the Nicola Water Use Management planning committee. She served on the Provincial Task Force on Species at Risk and as the president of the British Columbia Cattlemen's Association. She has also been a part of the Ranching Task Force for B.C. and the British Columbia Agri-Food Trade Advisory Council.

Andrew Heard

Dr. Andrew Heard is a professor in the political science department at Simon Fraser University and a past president of the British Columbia Political Studies Association. His research interests cover Canadian constitutional and institutional issues: the Crown, constitutional conventions, Senate reform, parliamentary privilege, federalism, elections, and the courts. He has published a second edition of *Canadian Constitutional Conventions: The Marriage of Law and Politics* (Toronto: Oxford University Press, 2014).

Rick W. Hill

Rick W. Hill Sr. is from the Tuscarora Nation, Beaver Clan. Curator, writer, artist, and storyteller, he is founding coordinator of Deyohahá:ge: The Indigenous Knowledge Centre at Six Nations Polytechnic, and distinguished fellow/adjunct professor at Mohawk College. He is the former assistant director for public programs, National Museum of the American Indian, Smithsonian Institution; museum director, Institute of American Indian Arts, Santa Fe, New Mexico; and assistant professor, Native American Studies, State University of New York at Buffalo. He recently retired as senior project coordinator of the Deyohahá:ge: Indigenous Knowledge Centre at Six Nations Polytechnic, Ohsweken, Ontario.

D. Michael Jackson, CVO, SOM, CD

Dr. Michael Jackson was chief of protocol for the Province of Saskatchewan from 1980 to 2005. He is author of *The Crown and Canadian Federalism* (Dundurn Press, 2013), co-editor of *The Evolving Canadian Crown* and of *Canada and the Crown: Essays on Constitutional Monarchy* (McGill-Queen's University Press, 2012, 2013), and editor of *The Canadian Kingdom: 150 Years of Constitutional Monarchy* (Dundurn Press, 2018). A Commander of the Royal Victorian Order and Member of the Saskatchewan Order of Merit, he is president of the Institute for the Study of the Crown in Canada.

David Johnson

Dr. David Johnson, a full professor at Cape Breton University, has been teaching political science for over twenty-five years, specializing in Canadian government and constitutional law and politics. His latest book is *Battle Royal: Monarchists vs. Republicans and the Crown of Canada* (Dundurn Press, 2018). His previous books include *Thinking Government: Public Administration and Politics in Canada*, 4th ed. (University of Toronto Press, 2017), and *Restraining Equality: Human Rights Commissions in Canada*, with Brian R. Howe (University of Toronto Press, 2000).

The Honourable Serge Joyal, PC, OC, OQ

The Honourable Serge Joyal has been a senator since 1997. He is the chair of the Standing Senate Committee on Legal and Constitutional Affairs, of which he has been a member for twenty years. He has been an MP, a minister, and Secretary of State, and in 1980–81 co-chaired the joint committee that recommended the adoption of the Canadian Charter of Rights and Freedoms. He has intervened in a personal capacity on a number of occasions before various Canadian courts to defend the recognition of rights and freedoms and the fundamental principles of parliamentary institutions. He is the author and publisher of several articles and books related to parliamentary and constitutional law, as well as essays in social and political history.

The Honourable Margaret McCain, CC, ONB

In 1994, Margaret Norrie McCain was appointed lieutenant governor of the province of New Brunswick — the first woman to hold this position. She served in that role until 1997, when she moved to Toronto. Mrs. McCain has been active in organizations that promote education, music, and the arts at the provincial and national levels. She served as chancellor of Mount Allison University from 1986 to 1994 and was a member of the board of the National Ballet School for eighteen years, serving as board chair from 1998 to 2000. She is currently chair of the Margaret & Wallace McCain Family Foundation. Mrs. McCain is patron of the Institute for the Study of the Crown in Canada.

Warren J. Newman

Dr. Warren J. Newman holds the office of Senior General Counsel in the Constitutional, Administrative and International Law Section of the Department of Justice of Canada. He has been a legal advisor to the Government of Canada and a practitioner of constitutional law for more than thirty-five years. A member of the Bars of Ontario and Quebec, Mr. Newman has acted as counsel for the Attorney General of Canada in several cases before the Supreme Court, including the *Manitoba Language Rights Reference*, the *Quebec Secession Reference*, and the *Senate Reform Reference*, as well as in cases before trial and appellate courts, including the *Motard* case on the *Succession to the Throne Act, 2013*. Mr. Newman has appeared on numerous occasions as an expert witness on legislative bills before parliamentary committees and is an adjunct professor and doctoral teaching fellow at the Faculties of Law of Queen's University, York University, and the University of Ottawa.

Dale Smith

Dale Smith is a freelance journalist in the Canadian Parliamentary Press Gallery, writing about politics full-time since the 2008 federal election, and author of *The Unbroken Machine: Canada's Democracy in Action* (Dundurn Press, 2017).

Nathan Tidridge, MSM

Nathan Tidridge teaches Canadian history, government, and Indigenous studies at Waterdown District High School, Ontario, and is author of Dundurn Press books *Canada's Constitutional Monarchy* (2011), *Prince Edward, Duke of Kent* (2013), and *The Queen at the Council Fire* (2015). He is a board member of the Ontario Heritage Trust and a member of the national advisory council for the Prince's Trust Canada. He was awarded the Meritorious Service Medal in 2018 for his work in educating Canadians on the role of the Crown and its relationship with Indigenous communities. He is vice-president of the Institute for the Study of the Crown in Canada.

IMAGE CREDITS

4 (*top &* *bottom*)   Rick W. Hill personal collection

15, 16, 22   Office of the Lieutenant Governor of Ontario

83, 89   Hon. Serge Joyal personal collection

95 (*left to* *right, top to* *bottom*)   National Capital Commission Official Residences Crown Collection: Lilias Torrance Newton; Charles Comfort; Charles Comfort; Jean Paul Lemieux; Irma Coucill; Cleeve Horne; Istvan Nikos; Christan Nicholson; Mary Pratt; Sgt. Eric Jolin, Rideau Hall © OSGG, 2007; Sgt. Ronald Duchesne, Rideau Hall © OSGG, 2015; Sgt. Johanie Maheu, Rideau Hall © OSGG, 2017

A Note on the Cover

Canada's Parliament has new thrones. They were commissioned to commemorate the 150th anniversary of Confederation and the first sitting of Parliament on November 6, 1867. These thrones are in the new Senate

Chamber and will be used while the Centre Block undergoes extensive renovation and modernization over the next ten years. Afterward, the new thrones will be offered to Rideau Hall for the use of the governor general. These impressive thrones are the first to be crafted since the creation of the oak neo-Gothic thrones made in 1878 for the Marquis of Lorne and his wife, Princess Louise, when he was appointed governor general. The new thrones are constructed of walnut and are based on the Pearson Arts and Crafts style used for furnishings of the Senate Chamber. Philip White, the Dominion Sculptor, prepared the actual design. They were constructed by Treebone Design and cabinet makers Ross Munro and Francis Camiré, with the sculptural elements carved by Alexandre Lepinsky; the upholsterer was Richard Soucy; and Isabelle Hordequin was responsible for the gilding. All are artisans from Montreal, Quebec.

What is particularly noteworthy is that the Queen supported the project. The prominent sculptural elements of the thrones are made from walnut harvested from the forest of the estate of Windsor Castle. The crowns of St. Edward and the gilded panels below embellished by maple leaves showing the royal cypher "ERII" on the sovereign's throne and the Canadian crest, and the crowned lion holding a maple leaf on the companion consort's throne are made from a plank of walnut given by the Queen.

The upholstered back of the thrones displays the shield of the Canadian coat of arms surrounded by a circlet with the motto of the Order of Canada in Latin, which translates as "Desiring a Better Country." The crossed stretchers below the seat of the thrones include gilded carvings of the English rose and the French *fleur-de-lys* to acknowledge the bicultural heritage of the country and the enduring legacy of monarchy since the French exploration of Canada in 1534.